Il Shri

The Secret o

tvameva mātā ca pitā tvameva
tvameva bandhuśca sakhā tvameva
tvameva vidyā draviṇaṁ tvameva
tvameva sarvaṁ mama devadeva

त्वमेव माता च पिता त्वमेव
त्वमेव बन्धुश्च सखा त्वमेव।
त्वमेव विद्या द्रविणं त्वमेव
त्वमेव सर्वं मम देवदेव॥

Jayadayal Goyandka

[521] S. of P. 1/A

Ninth Reprint 2009 2,000
Total 32,000

❖ **Price : Rs. 10**
(Ten Rupees only)

ISBN 81-293-0044-3

Printed & Published by :
Gita Press, Gorakhpur—273005 (INDIA)
(a unit of Gobind Bhavan-Karyalaya, Kolkata)
Phone - (0551) 2334721; Fax - (0551) 2336997
e-mail : **booksales@gitapress.org** website : **www.gitapress.org**

[521] S. of P. 1/B

॥ Śrī Hari ॥

Publisher's Note

It is a matter of great pleasure to me to submit this book 'The Secret of Premayoga' to our readers. Brahmalīna Late Shri Jayadayal Goyandaka does not require introduction to the followers of spiritual discipline. He was an exalted soul, a devotee of the highest order who was blessed with divine vision even during his life-time.

Present book is a compilation of 16 articles written by him and published in the Kalyana-Kalpataru from time to time. It is a valuable and useful book particularly for those aspirants who are striving to realise God and obtain His blessing through Bhakti-Mārga or the path of love and devotion. It can serve the purpose of a true guide to the Sādhakas on this path, toddling and trying.

Shri Goyandakaji was not a man of theory but he practically lived those principles and lines which he has propounded in these articles.

Gopīs' unalloyed love was his ideal and a pollar star to him. Self-surrender was another technique, though of a bit grosser nature yet quite effective. In the 9th article Shri Goyandakaji has almost chalked out an exhaustive plan for developing love towards the Lord which can be very beneficial to the beginners and so is article 12th which discusses the Means of Developing love for God.

The third important thing to Shri Goyandakaji was Satsaṅga. To the followers of Bhakti-Mārga, 'Satsaṅga' means the company of Bhaktas only; company of Mīrās, Sūras and Tulasīs.

The article 8th narrates the story of Pravīra which glorifies the wonderful devotion of Pravīra who defeated Arjuna at every step—even by being killed he defeated him. An ideal devotee of Lord Kṛṣṇa. It is a most thrilling story worth reading.

To cut it short, the book is in the hands of the readers. It was a standing demand from some friends to publish these precious notes in the book form which could materialise after a prolonged waiting. We hope our readers will generously excuse us for any shortcomings, commissions and omissions for which we must shoulder the responsibility.

I have received much needed co-operation and help from many corners for which I express my gratitude to all of them. We will feel our endeavour fruitful if this book renders any service to those who are fellow travellers on the path of Bhakti.

॥ Śrī Hari ॥

CONTENTS

★

Divine Love and Self-Surrender

The character of Divine Love can never be truly described. It makes the devotee the very embodiment of Love. It is like the sweet tasted by the dumb. The joy of Divine Love also is indescribable. Horripilation, tears, trembling of the body, etc., are only external signs of it; but how is one to give expression to the stream of Rasa (delight) that flows interminably within the heart ? The stream overflows and floods the heart. We read the stories of Love-intoxicated devotees, but in the present age the sight of a true Lover of God has become extremely rare. Even a single true Lover of God can sanctify and redeem crores of beings.

A showering cloud will moisten the earth to whichever direction, it may move. Even so the Lover of God moistens all movable and immovable objects of creation through the shower of Divine Love. The very sight of the Divine Lover brings a new life to the heart and makes it bloom like a flower. The great saint Tulasīdāsajī says:—

"It is my belief, O Lord, that a servant of Rāma is greater than even Rāma Himself.

*Rāma is like the ocean, the saint is like the cloud; Rāma is the sandal tree and the saint is the breeze."**

Drawing water from the ocean the cloud showers it below and thus confers immense good on all creatures. God is the ocean and the saint the cloud. Drawing his store of Divine Love from God Himself the saint showers it on earth. Again, just as the rain-water trickling through earth enters canals, streams and rivers and thus fertilizing the earth winds its way finally to the ocean, even so the saint sending down showers of Divine Love, finally surrenders that Love to the source of Love, God Himself.

* मोरें मन प्रभु अस बिस्वासा। राम ते अधिक राम कर दासा॥
राम सिंधु घन सज्जन धीरा। चंदन तरु हरि संत समीरा॥

The Lord is the sandal tree and the saint the breeze. Just as the breeze spreads the sweet smell of the sandal to distant regions, even so the saint spreads the divine scent of the Lord. The sight of the saint brings the Lord to recollection. Therefore, the saint is an image of the Lord. Just as the peasant and the Cātaka bird live depending on the cloud, similarly the man of faith lives depending exclusively on the saint.

The voice and eyes of the Lover of God pours down Love. He sends a stream of Love through the road he passes. The very dust and breeze of the place he sanctifies by his presence begin to reflect Love and only Love. His very touch is full of Love, full of kindness and affection.

Now, the question is—how is one to gain this Love ? Gosvāmī Tulasīdāsajī says in answer to this question:—

"Without satsaṅga discourses on the stories of Śrī Hari cannot be heard, and without hearing such discourse delusion cannot be removed.

*Until delusion is removed, strong attachment to the feet of Śrī Rāma cannot be developed."**

The tragedy is that all our attachments are rooted to wealth and woman, honour and fame. We do not, in fact, entertain any desire in our hearts to gain true Divine Love. Until the heart thirsts for this Love, feels intensely agitated, how is it possible for one to gain it ? We are in the stage now when our lustful mind finds delight and joy in the love for woman. Our greedy heart is mad in its pursuit of wealth. The fickle mind constantly runs after honour and fame. Until this lust and greed are all withdrawn from worldly objects, and the energies they represent are sent towards God, how is it possible for us to gain Divine Love ?

The true Lover of God speaks even through silence. All his limbs tend, as if, to participate in this speech. From every part of his body emanates an influence and a note of purity. The Divine Lover does not go anywhere to preach. What will he speak, and

* बिनु सतसंग न हरि कथा तेहि बिनु मोह न भाग।
मोह गएँ बिनु राम पद होइ न दृढ़ अनुराग॥

how will he give expression to it ? When, and to whom, did the Gopīs go to teach the ways of Love ? When, and to whom, did Bharatajī speak about Bhakti ? His very character remains, and will forever remain, as a living exposition on Bhakti. The Gopīs are the very embodiments of the spirit of self-surrender and exclusiveness of Love, which are so highly valued in Divine Love. Similarly, in the *Rāmāyaṇa* , the Love-laden form of Śrī Bharatajī stands as the very soul of it.

This body of ours is the Kṣetra or field. Whatever seed in the form of Karma you sow in this field such crop you will get from it in return. The best seed is the Japa of the Divine Name alongwith loving meditation on the Form of the Paramātmā. Without water, however the seed does not germinate. Water in this case is the discourse on Śrī Hari and Divine Grace. A field in which wheat has been sown will yield wheat, where mango is cultivated will yield mangoes, and where Rāma (God) is sown will yield Rāma. If we go on throwing seeds in the form of Japa and meditation on God, we shall attain God, the repository of Love. Direct realization of God is, in fact, the crop of this seed. An ordinary seed when thrown on earth sometimes gets destroyed, but the immortal seed of the Name of Rāma taken even disinterestedly will never be destroyed. Discourses on Śrī Hari and Divine Grace constitute water, which one can draw only from the association of saints. Pure Love for God develops through such discourses and Divine Grace. Therefore, association of saints is the means of acquiring Divine Love.

How shall we develop this Love for the Lord ? Take the instance of Śrī Rāma. While searching for Sītā, He asked even the trees and creepers—"Have you seen My beloved Sītā ?" Take, again, the instance of the Gopīs who roamed from one forest to another in search of the jewel of their hearts shouting all the while 'Kṛṣṇa'. In Love, the greater the intensity of yearning, the quicker does God bless the Sādhaka with His realization.

Again, God is realized only when the thought begins constantly to trouble the Sādhaka—"How is God quickly to be attained ?" This yearning should go on increasing. Intense yearning is the cause which makes the Beloved Lord reveal Himself. He is realized only through Love. Love grows from a knowledge of His secret and glory. When we gain even a slight knowledge of His secret, it will be impossible for us to live without Him even for a moment.

When the Cātaka bird sees a cloud in the sky it loses consciousness of the external world in the intensity of its yearning. Let us similarly turn mad for the sake of the Lord. Let us begin every moment to feel life unbearable without Him.

Let our Love for the Lord be of the type as entertained by the fish for water, by the Cātaka for the cloud and by the Cakora for the moon. Let us not even for a moment feel at ease without Him. This type of Love can be developed only through the grace of saints, who are themselves embodiments of Love. Carrying scent from the sandal tree the breeze transforms the timber of all nearby trees into sandal. Though it is the scent which brings about this transformation, without the breeze it cannot spread. It is thus the saints who showering the Bliss of the Lord make the world full of Bliss, or bring a flood in the ocean of Love and Bliss. To whichever direction Gourāṅga Mahāprabhu went during his peregrinations he would make the stream of Divine Love flow as if in a flood. What a great store of nectar is the writings of Gosvāmī Tulasīdāsajī ! The sight of great saints of this type becomes possible only through the grace of God. This grace though showered equally on all does not produce its fruitful effect unless the instrument is ready. The devotee who has taken refuge in the Lord is such a fit instrument. Therefore let us place ourselves under the protection of the Lord and surrender ourselves completely from all points of view to His sacred feet. The Lord also says:—

"O Arjuna, take complete refuge under Him(God). By His grace you will attain Supreme Peace and His Eternal Abode." *

Surrender should be made through mind, speech and action. Then alone it will become complete. In other words, attempt

* तमेव शरणं गच्छ सर्वभावेन भारत।
तत्प्रसादात्परां शान्तिं स्थानं प्राप्स्यसि शाश्वतम्॥

(*Gītā* XVIII. 62)

should be made to be with God through the mind, through speech as well as through action.

To remain contented with whatever may be ordained by God and to engage the mind in the remembrance of His Name, Form, Virtues and Sports is living with God through the mind. To utter His Names and sing His glories is to live with Him through Karma, or action.

Mentally Living with God

(1) A genuine devotee sees only His mercy through every incident ordained by God, and feels God to be an ocean of mercy and justice. He regards God alone to be the best lover and truest friend. Justice is involved in His mercy, and mercy in His justice. Everything appears to him as a boon from God. Death also is a mark of His compassion. How great was the joy of Mayūradhvaja's son when he learnt that his flesh would be served as food to Śrī Kṛṣṇa's lion. The devotee welcomes even death with outstretched arms regarding it as a blessing from God. Taking it as a boon from God, he feels joy and sees his highest good to be served by it. Like an expert actor and dissembler, God always and everywhere moves concealed both within and without us. He who realizes this Truth sees everywhere His mercy and mercy alone.

When one thus surrenders oneself to Him, he will feel joy and nothing but joy through every divine dispensation. Even a kick from the Beloved will appear exceptionally delicious. It is sweeter than His endearment and the shoes with which He kicks will appear to be surcharged with an exceptional sweetness.

(2) Writing mentally the Names of the Lord on a wall, on the heart or on an image, to engage the mind in their repetition is the practice of remembrance of the Divine Name.

(3) To meditate on God's existence everywhere like the ether in the form of Saccidānanda (Existence, Knowledge and Bliss) is meditation on the Formless, Absolute state of God. That Paramātmā Himself, the repository of Knowledge and Bliss, assumes a Divine Form through His Yogamāyā, and reveals Himself as celestial beings, men and other forms of beings—realizing this, to meditate on His sweet Divine Form is meditation

on the Lord as Personal God. Just as the whole truth about water is known only by him who knows it in the form of atom in a clear sky, cloud, rain and hail, even so he who knows the Absolute and Personal aspects of the Lord knows His Integral Form. In Chapter VII of the *Gītā,* the Lord has given a detailed exposition on this Truth. True meditation lies in meditation on the Lord after unravelling this secret.

(4) The Lord is an ocean of all Sāttvika qualities. His forbearance, compassion, tranquillity, equal-mindedness, simplicity, generosity and purity are unlimited. Knowledge, dispassion, brilliance and glory have their fullest manifestation in Him. The compassion and Love that are observed in all the beings of creation cannot together equal even a drop of the Love and compassion of that Ocean of Compassion

The brilliance and Knowledge of the whole world when brought together cannot equal the brilliance of even an insignificant fraction of Paramātmā, the repository of all brilliance and Knowledge. Thus to reflect on all the qualities of the Lord is meditation on His virtues and qualities.

(5) Manifesting Himself in a human form as the son of King Daśaratha, the Lord has left for us lessons of rectitude and Love through His ideal conduct towards His brothers. Carrying out the order of exile passed by His parents, He has taught us the spirit of service. He chastised the wicked and relieved the distress of Ṛṣis, Munis and virtuous souls. He looked after His subjects with affectionate care undergoing much sacrifice for their sake. By His practices of sacrifice, charity, austerity, service, truth, Brahmacarya and other forms of virtuous conduct, He has left object-lessons for our guidance. Thus to reflect on His sacred Character is meditation on the Līlās (sports) of the Lord.

Practice of Living with God through Speech

Japa of the Lord's Names and Mantras connected with the Lord, recitation of hymns, Kīrtana of the Lords' Names and glories, explaining to fellow-devotees the Name, Form, Virtues, Love and Power of the Lord, to discuss mutually among friends only about God, to speak with humility what is true and dear—thus to engage the organ of speech only to utterance of things connected with the Lord is what is called practice of living with God through speech.

Living with God through Action

One should perform disinterestedly the duties of life only for the sake of the Lord, according to the Lord's desire and behest. Just as a devoted wife carries out the direction of the husband for the sake of the husband, even so he should carry out the instructions of the Lord.

In order to please its master the monkey in a travelling show dances, jumps and plays, other pranks just as its master bids it do. We are also like monkeys under the control of the Divine Magician and whatever pleases Him should please us also. That flower is, indeed,blessed which gains the privilege of being placed at the feet of the Lord, and that life is blessed which is offered as a sacrifice unto the Lord !

An owner of a piece of cloth may wear it, may spread it on his bed, may tear it or burn it down to ashes; the cloth is prepared for everything. The attitude of the devotee also should be similar to this. Whether the Lord delivers him, chastises him, breaks or burns him, the devotee submits completely to His will. He should ever feel delighted observing the guiding hand of the Lord in every circumstance of life.

We are mere puppets in the hands of the Lord and should dance as He bids us dance. It is our supreme duty to remain satisfied surrendering ourselves to the will of the Lord.

To perform sacrifices, charity, austerities, and other virtuous deeds, and observe Brahmacarya, seeing everywhere the presence of God, and while rendering service to all creatures to treat them with humility and love is what may be called living with God through action.

Bear it in mind, on taking refuge with the Lord, even an evil turns out to be good:—

"Poison becomes like nectar, and an enemy turns into a friend." *

If one even dies after taking refuge with the Lord, that death of his is superior to the attainment of salvation. The Lord says—

* गरल सुधा सम अरि हित होई ।

*"I ruin him, who seeks Me; and become his bond slave, if he does not renounce Me even after he is ruined."**

The devotee who thus surrenders himself to the Lord becomes a proper object of His grace and through that grace he succeeds in gaining immaculate Divine Love and attains supreme peace and supreme bliss through a direct vision of the Lord.

Therefore, we should kick away from our path all objects of worldly enjoyment and take refuge only in the Lord. We should also withdraw the mind from pursuit of desires for prosperity and possession of supernatural powers, for honour, fame and social status. This world is like an unfathomable ocean. There are two ways of crossing it—(1) by a boat, and (2) by swimming. Practice of Divine Love constitutes the boat for crossing this ocean and practice of Sāṅkhyayoga or Jñāna (Knowledge) constitutes the act of swimming. It is needless to point out that to sail by boat on this ocean is easier, safer and more certain of taking us to the other shore than the attempt to cross it by swimming.

In order to get the boat in the form of Divine Love one should take refuge in the Lord. For the attempt to swim across what is required is courage and power of renunciation. In the act of swimming one has to strike his hands and feet against the water and constantly move forward. In this ocean of existence we may swim by striking our hands and feet against water in the form of worldly objects, provided we do not lose sight of the goal of reaching the other shore and do not allow the waves to hold up and exhaust our hands and feet. At the time of swimming there should be no burden on the body. Thus to advance cutting our way through the waves in the form of worldly objects we require determination in the form of strong dispassion, without which it will be impossible to advance even a yard. The hands should cut through the waves and the feet should strike against the water.

Renunciation of objects of enjoyment is indispensible in true surrender. It is impossible for both attachment for objects of enjoyment and surrender to God to remain side by side.

---

* जे करे आमार आस, ताँर करि सर्वनास।
तबु जे छाँड़े ना आस, ताँर हई दासेर दास॥

The desire for name and fame is a subtler and more obstinate obstacle than even the desire for wealth and woman. It entangles in its net even men who are great in the field of spiritual attainment, retards their progress and eventually drowns many of them. It should be always carefully guarded against.

There is not the least doubt that instead of swimming with the help of knowledge, it is more comfortable, easier and more delightful to cross the ocean by boarding the boat of Divine Love which is eternally new.

This immaculate Love can be gained only through exclusive surrender to the Lord, therefore exclusive surrender is the equivalent of journey by a boat. The crossing of this ocean of existence is indispensable in any case. Without reaching the other shore vision of the Beloved can never be obtained. Then, why not take refuge in Him and proceed on the journey with His help ? The Lord Himself promises:—

"O Arjuna, devotees who offering all their actions to Me, worship Me meditating on Me as Personal God, as incessantly as the flow of oil, these I speedily lift up and save from the ocean of existence and death, their minds being fixed on Me." *

This ocean of existence is very difficult, indeed, to cross, and the easiest method of crossing it is to take refuge in the Lord. The Lord says:—

"This extraordinary divine illusion (Yogamāyā) of Mine, consisting of the three Guṇas, is very difficult to get over. He who engages himself in constant adoration of Me, crosses it." †

We should, therefore, take exclusive refuge‡ in the Lord, through mind, speech and action for gaining Divine Love and for the realization of God, who is the very embodiment of Love.

* ये तु सर्वाणि कर्माणि मयि संन्यस्य मत्पराः। अनन्येनैव योगेन मां ध्यायन्त उपासते॥
तेषामहं समुद्धर्ता मृत्युसंसारसागरात्। भवामि नचिरात्पार्थ मय्यावेशितचेतसाम्॥
(*Gītā* XII. 6-7)

† दैवी ह्येषा गुणमयी मम माया दुरत्यया। मामेव ये प्रपद्यन्ते मायामेतां तरन्ति ते॥
(*Gītā* VII. 14)

‡ Adoration through inseparable union, unadulterated devotion, and exclusive refuge in the Lord mean one and the same thing.

The Practice of Divine Love

The fulfilment of life lies in the growth of exclusive Love for Bhagavān Śrī Kṛṣṇa the beloved Prince of Vraja. The fortunate soul who has drunk of this nectar of pure, undeviating Love, has reached the true object of life. The thirst for objective happiness from which he has been suffering, life after life, and from age to age, at last meets with satisfaction and comes to an end. Distressed by the heat of suffering of worldly existence, man can attain total peace only by taking a plunge in the sacred waters of the Ganges of Divine Love. This is that supreme Rasa (spiritual elixir), having drunk which man attains perfection, immortality and complete satisfaction;* having gained which he rises above the world of desire and sorrow, of attraction and repulsion and begins to float in an infinite, unfathomable ocean of joy. Then, he does no longer enjoy sense-objects, nor finds pleasure in such enjoyment.†

Divine Love in both the means (as practice), and the end or fruit of such practice.‡ Like God Himself, Divine Love also is indescribable; it cannot be an object of speech, like the taste enjoyed by the dumb.§ That is why this Love is described as something supernatural, for there is nothing in the world which can be likened to it. Worldly love, because it is tainted by evil desires, the desires of enjoyment, is not pure love. Where desire reigns supreme, there can be no love; it is a form of fascination of which attachment is the root. Besides, the object of worldly love

---

* यल्लब्ध्वा सिद्धो भवति, अमृतो भवति, तृप्तो भवति।

(*Nārada Bhakti-Sūtras* 4)

† यत्प्राप्य न किञ्चिद्वाञ्छति न शोचति न द्वेष्टि न रमते नोत्साही भवति।

(*Nārada Bhakti-Sūtras* 5)

‡ साधन सिद्धि राम-पग नेहू।

§ अनिर्वचनीयं प्रेमस्वरूपम्। मूकास्वादनवत्।

(*Bhakti-Sūtras* 51-52)

is transient, perishable; therefore, it is bound to be worthless when compared to Divine Love. Divine Love, again, when cultivated with the motive of gaining worldly desire is called Love with motive. The divine element, as well as exclusiveness and purity, must be lacking in this Love. Desire is cultivated for worldly objects; and the mixture of worldliness in Love destroys its divine character. Again, the desires making a free run on Love distribute it among themselves, that is why there remains no exclusiveness in worldly love. Similarly, the purity of Love is lost when it is mixed up with desires. Divine, exclusive and pure Love is a state which is beyond the modes of the Guṇas and wholly free from the region of desires; it continues to grow from moment to moment and knows no diminution; it is subtler than the subtlest experience; it cannot be expressed through speech. It is only an object of experience.

Motive or desire vitiates Love. Motiveless, disinterested Love, because it is not tainted by desire, is pure Love. Except dearest Śrī Kṛṣṇa, the Paramātmā, who is identical with the Self, there is no other object of this Love; hence this Love is exclusive. And it is divine, because it transcends the region of the Guṇas as stated above.

The fortunate soul who gains this Love remains intoxicated by it, and knows no break in his intoxication. Worldly thoughts cannot even touch his mind. In his view nothing remains but Love. What he sees is Love, what he hears is Love, what he speaks or thinks upon is Love. His mind, breath and soul are constantly merged in the Ganges flow of Love. He offers all his duties and activities to the dearest object of Love, Śrī Kṛṣṇa. He feels supremely miserable and restless at the slightest lapse in His remembrance. Everywhere he sees God, the object of his Love, and sees everything in God. God can never move out from the eyesight of a devotee who cultivates this vision, nor can such a devotee ever separate himself from God.

Thus continues their eternal union, the everlasting state of the two becoming one. Observing this supernatural Love of the devotee, God forgets that He is the mighty overlord of creation and moved by affection Himself begins to gaze and gaze at the beloved devotee, and assuming a Form according to the conception and desire of the devotee sports with him, dances, sings, plays on musical instruments and makes merry with him.

The devotee, who is a true lover of God, rises even above the thoughts of union and separation. What interest has he that he should be overwhelmed with grief for union ? He is interested only in offering his love, and that also love for love's sake. The Beloved, who is a Master in the art of Love, cannot Himself remain indifferent to such a devotee. If He has any business, He will Himself come to the devotee. why should the latter trouble himself with the thought of union ? And why should he be afraid of separation ? He does not seek any joy or happiness for himself; what he does is for the happiness of the Beloved. If the Beloved feels happy through union, let Him come Himself. If separation causes him misery, let Him not go anywhere else. The fact of the matter is God possesses inordinate greed for Love; where there is Love, He will Himself make haste to come; and where there is no Love, He will not care to go even if He is importuned with repeated emphasis and earnestness. This is the reason why those who cultivate Divine Love in a disinterested spirit, do not call on God to come to them. In fact, it is neither necessary to appeal to God to reveal Himself, nor prevent Him from doing so. What is truly necessary is to increase one's Love for Him without any interest or motive. All one's energy and effort should be concentrated on increasing this Love from more to more, keeping egoism and pride at a distance and remaining indifferent to the thoughts of union and separation. Prahlāda never prayed, 'Oh Lord, favour me with Your sight'. What had to be done for him was done by God Himself.

All activities of the devotee in the path of Divine Love from the act of worship down to ordinary acts like taking of food, etc., must be performed with the sole object of pleasing God. Except God, the object of his Love, there should be nothing in the view of the Divine Lover. The vision of God, or union with God, these are but accessory results, which will be automatically realized. The complete fruition of this Love lies in the realization of identity between the Lover, Love and the object of Love.

A Lover who has realized this state becomes the very embodiment of Divine Love. His speech becomes permeated with Love, his body and mind appear to be merged in the delicious juice of Love. The very hairs of his body will appear to dance in the joy of Love. Through conversation with him, meditation on him and approaching near him, one may imbibe the air of Love, and his touch will bring a flood of Love even in a dry and withered heart. Coming in contact with him, even great atheists may forget their atheism and turn mad in the path of Love.

There are no proper words to convey with correctness, the experience of this exclusive and transcendent Love. The analogy of sentiments of the world is no doubt used to express it, but in that state, there is neither sentiment, nor want of sentiment. It is a state much above all sentiments.

Divine Love cannot be compared even to the friendly sentiment. It is something superior to the sentiment of a friend. Arjuna is considered to be a representative devotee who cultivated the friendly sentiment; but even in Arjuna deficiency is observed in respect of this transcendent Love. He gets frightened at the sight of the Lord's Universal Form. He begins to feel that he committed a terrible guilt by treating the Lord on the equal terms of a friend and is found to be craving for the Lord's pardon, again and again:—

'तत्क्षामये त्वामहमप्रमेयम् ।'
'पितेव पुत्रस्य सखेव सख्युः
प्रियः प्रियायार्हसि देव सोढुम् ॥'

And the Lord also comforts him by saying—(मा ते व्यथा मा च विमूढभावः)

"Do not be afraid, do not be bewildered."

Exclusive Divine Love is superior even to the servant-sentiment. In the servant-sentiment, there are ideas of high and low, of master and servant; but in that state there reigns complete equality, neither there is any servant, nor any master. The devotee feels delighted by plunging into the Ganges of Divine Love, and God also similarly gets absorbed in Love.

The stage of exclusive Divine Love is superior even to the parent-sentiment. In the parent-sentiment that transcendent equality is not discovered, which is an ordinary object of experience in Divine Love. In the parent-sentiment ideas of superiority and inferiority, of father and son, continue; but in exclusive Love neither is one inferior, nor superior, neither is one mother or father, nor son. In that region all are equal.

This extraordinary Love is different even from the sweet Lover-sentiment. There are two aspects of the Lover-sentiment—(1) the sentiment of the wedded wife, and (2) the sentiment of the paramour. The love borne by the ideal, chaste wife towards her husband is the measure of the wifely sentiment. And the paramour-sentiment towards the Divine Being is to be understood on the analogy of the illicit and secret love borne by an unchaste woman towards her paramour. The Divine Lover lives on a plane which is higher than and superior to all these sentiments. He does not suffer the pang of separation from God even for a moment. God becomes, in fact, subordinate to him, remaining always at his beck and call. God never goes anywhere leaving that devotee alone. That exclusive Divine Lover becomes the complete embodiment of Love—he remains, within and without, full of God. He is not separate from God, nor is God separate from him. In that state there is neither fear nor reserve, and considerations like showing of honour and respect do not arise at all. No difference is shown on the ground of one being superior and the other inferior. In between God and His devotee, none is superior and none is inferior. Both of them are equal.

A devoted wife looks upon her husband as Nārāyaṇa, the Supreme Puruṣa and considers herself to be His female servant.

This sentiment is very high and very helpful for spiritual growth. But in this also there is differentiation of high and low. But in exclusive Divine Love there is no such differentiation. In that state both occupy the same status—both are on the same level.

In the paramour-sentiment, there is fear of others, there is the tendency to conceal the clandestine love and an anxiety that it may not come to light, but in transcendent Divine Love there is no place for fear or the desire of concealment, no place for nervousness at all. The devotee cultivating this sentiment feels attracted by God's glory and power; where there is the feeling of superiority of another, there must be a corresponding feeling of deficiency in one's own self. Therefore, this state also lacks fearlessness and a sense of complete equality. But in exclusive and pure Love, there is no consciousness of glory and power; in fact, they are considered to be of no value, even if the mind may be occasionally conscious of their existence. This stage represents an indescribable union between the two. In this stage, the devotee does not offer prayers calling God as Almighty and the Knower of all hearts. The stage of prayer is passed long before reaching this state. Now, the ideas of almightiness and overlordship of God lose all meaning; the devotee and the Lord become one and equal, both are Lovers and both are Beloved; the Love between them becomes wholly motiveless and natural. Love, Lover and the Beloved lose all distinction in this stage. The Devotee, Devotion and the object of Devotion (God)—all become one. This is corroborated by the following outpouring of a devotee in the path of Love—

त्रिधाप्येकं सदा गम्यं गम्यमेकप्रभेदने ।
प्रेम प्रेमी प्रेमपात्रं त्रितयं प्रणतोऽस्म्यहम् ॥

"Love, Lover and the Beloved, though appearing three, are one. The truth about them cannot be always understood by all. They should be looked upon as one whole. I offer my obeisance to these three, who are in reality one."

In the eye of such an exclusive Divine Lover, the world will appear as full of the luminous light of transcendent Divine Love.

He will shower the nectar of Love on all irrespective of any consideration. In his view, none will appear as an object of hatred or repulsion. Under all circumstances, he will feel the ocean of Love throwing up its unending waves.

The Mahātmā following the path of Knowledge realizes Brahma through the establishment of identity with Brahma, 'ब्रह्मैव सन् ब्रह्माप्येति'. But in this transcendent world of Divine Love, the experience is something different. There is neither duality, nor non-duality here. It is a peculiar state different from both the states. The evernew Love between the Lover and Beloved goes on increasing from more to more (प्रतिक्षणं वर्धमानम्). It becomes boundless and infinite. The devotee and the Lord become so united that they lose all sense of duality. Words cannot describe the experience of this transcendent state. Nothing except Love is the object of experience in that state. The meeting between two Divine Lovers also exposes to view a unique and unforgettable sight. Although they are one, they appear two; and though appearing two, they are as a matter of fact one. When we join our palms, they become one though they are two, and they are two even though they become one. Similarly, between Divine Lovers there is neither difference, nor non-difference.

When the Ganges falls into the ocean, they together become one. The transcendent union between God and His lover-devotee is superior even to this. It is an indescribable state, the fruit of all endeavours, beyond the states of duality and non-duality. This union is eternal.

In this state, the separation caused by clothes, ornaments, weapons, etc., also appears to be undesirable. Clothes are used to cover one's shame, and the sense of shame is felt only with reference to another. Here the Lover and the Beloved have become one in spirit. Does anyone feel shame in his own presence ? In a closed room where one is alone one does not feel it necessary to cover oneself up with clothes and maintain a decent appearance. In this Divine union all duality has ceased, and the two appear separate only in the eyes of others. In this union ornaments also appear as hindrances, and there is no external show of honour, respect and courtesy. Honour and courtesy have no place where Love is complete. Does anyone show courtesy to one's own self ? This state is reached as the fruit of Love practised by Gopīs.

In this state, there will be no trace of any mental modification like grief, fear and delusion, etc.—the duality will lie only in appearance, but in reality union will be complete. Whatever the external behaviour of a devotee who has attained exclusive Love may be, internally he is thoroughly united, he is mentally merged in God, and is, therefore, eternally established in God. The Lord says in the *Gītā*—

सर्वभूतस्थितं यो मां भजत्येकत्वमास्थितः ।
सर्वथा वर्तमानोऽपि स योगी मयि वर्तते ॥

(VI.31)

"He who established in unity, worships Me as residing in all beings, that Yogī, though engaged in all forms of activities, dwells in Me."

This is an indescribable state beyond duality and non-duality, beyond separation and identity. The true goal of life of every human being is to attain this exclusive Love for Bhagavān Śrī Kṛṣṇa, the beloved Prince of Vraja. The fruition of life lies in attaining this.

Divine Incarnation

An incarnation of God, or descent of the Divine, means appearance of God from an unmanifest to a manifest state. It is an extremely uncommon, an esoteric matter. Therefore, he who comes to know this divine secret of the descent of God attains God Himself (*v. Gītā* IV.9).

God, the Supreme Brahma, the ocean of grace, takes an incarnation out of motiveless compassion to all, and for the supreme good of the world; in other words, He actually takes birth. The greatness of God is so infinite that even the Demiurge, Brahmā, feels himself incompetent to describe His glory. In the *Bhāgavata,* Śrī Brahmā says:—

सुरेष्वृषिष्वीश तथैव नृष्वपि
तिर्यक्षु यादस्स्वपि तेऽजनस्य ।
जन्मासतां दुर्मदनिग्रहाय
प्रभो विधातः सदनुग्रहाय च ॥
को वेत्ति भूमन् भगवन् परात्मन्
योगेश्वरोतीर्भवतस्त्रिलोक्याम् ।
क्व वा कथं वा कति वा कदेति
विस्तारयन्क्रीडसि योगमायाम् ॥

(X. xiv.20-21)

"O Lord, O Ruler of the Universe, O Providence, You are unborn, yet when You incarnate Yourself among Devas, Ṛṣīs, men or animals, whether moving on land or aquatic, You do so in order to chastise the wicked and confer Your blessings on the virtuous. O Lord, You are the all-pervading Supreme Soul, the Lord of Yoga; when You spread Your Yogamāyā and engage Yourself in sports, who is there in the three worlds who can penetrate the mystery and realize where, when, in what manner and in how many forms You are sporting ?"

What can be a greater mark of His grace on Jīvas, that this very God in order to play with us, comes down on earth assuming a

Form similar to that of ours ? He is verily an ocean of grace. It is His very nature to confer His grace. He cannot do without scattering grace. That is why when His devotees are faced with difficulties and dangers, when the earth weighs down through the burden of sins, when the virtuous are persecuted and the tyranny of the tyrant becomes unbearable, He has to come down from time to time and manifest Himself on earth to remove the earth's burden, to redeem His devotees and establish righteousness on earth by the protection of the virtuous and repression of the wicked. The Lord Himself says in the *Gītā*:—

अजोऽपि सन्नव्ययात्मा भूतानामीश्वरोऽपि सन्।
प्रकृतिं स्वामधिष्ठाय सम्भवाम्यात्ममायया ॥
यदा यदा हि धर्मस्य ग्लानिर्भवति भारत।
अभ्युत्थानमधर्मस्य तदात्मानं सृजाम्यहम् ॥
परित्राणाय साधूनां विनाशाय च दुष्कृताम्।
धर्मसंस्थापनार्थाय संभवामि युगे युगे ॥

(IV.6—8)

"Though unborn and unperishable, and also the Lord of all beings, I manifest Myself wielding My Nature (Prakṛti) through My own Yogamāyā (enrapturing power). Whenever there is decline of righteousness, and unrighteousness is on the ascendency, O descendant of Bharata, then I body forth Myself. For the protection of the virtuous, for the annihilation of evil-doers, and for the sake of establishing Dharma (righteousness) on a firm footing, I am born from age to age."

Here, the question arises—God is almighty, all-powerful, He is capable of doing everything; without coming down as an Avatāra He can have things done by His own inherent power, by His mere thought; where is, then, the need for His appearing on earth as an Avatāra ? The logic of the question is perfectly right. Yes, without taking any incarnation, God could do everything, He can do everything, and as a matter of fact, He does everything; and yet He takes a Form and appears (on earth out of special compassion) for people to give them, through His sight, His touch and His speech, an opportunity to liberate themselves easily from bondage, and give His loving devotees the taste of joy of His divine sports. People cross the ocean of existence with ease through the hearing, Kīrtana and remembrance of the virtues, powers, glories, Names, Forms and sports of God in those incarnations. This could not be possible without the Lord's descent on earth. This is the reason why He appears on earth as an Avatāra.

The second question arises—How is it possible for God, who is all-pervading in His Formless, Absolute state, to appear like a finite object in a limited portion of space ? And if He does so, He must be, for the time being, absent in other parts of space, and His powers must get extremely circumscribed. With a view to understand the answer to this question we should take the instance of fire in its unmanifest and manifest states. In its formless, state, fire is all-pervading, that is why it can anywhere be brought into manifestation by a piece of flint, or by striking a match, or by any other means. And when brought into manifestation at a particular place, its presence in other places is not negated; on the contrary, it is found manifested at several places at one and the same time. And wherever it appears, it retains all its powers. According to this analogy, although remaining all-pervading in His Formless, absolute state, God appears in a particular place in all His Divine glory, and when He does so, His presence is not thereby negated in other places. The scriptures mention several instances of His appearing simultaneously at various places. In describing Bhagavān Śrī Kṛṣṇa's visit to Mithilā, the *Bhāgavata* says that the King of Mithilā, Bahulāśva by name, was an exclusive devotee of the Lord. In the same town resided another Brāhmaṇa devotee of the Lord, Śrutadeva by name. Both of them prayed to the Lord together to grace their respective houses with His visit. In devotion both of them were unique in their own ways; the Lord did not want to hurt the feelings of any of them. Therefore, in order to please both of them, He assumed two forms without their knowledge and simultaneously appeared in both the houses* and graced them. There is another instance mentioned in the *Śrīmad Bhāgavata*. Devarṣi Nārada, being curious how the Lord carried on His duties as a householder, once came to Dvārakā and began to visit the palaces of the queens one after another. In every palace, He found Śrī Kṛṣṇa present, engaged in the proper performance of one or another household duty. Assuming many Forms, the Lord used to perform carefully in every palace all the regular daily duties of a householder, from early in the morning till late at night. When going to the Sabhā Hall, He used to appear coming out of the different palaces in many Forms and then becoming one Form entered the Hall. Seeing all these supernatural activities, Devarṣi Nārada was struck with wonder, and bowing to the feet of the Lord, He left for Brahmaloka, singing the Lord's praises *(Bhāgavata* X. ixix 13—43).

In connection with the delusion of Brahmā, the *Bhāgavata,* again, says that the Lord Himself assumed the forms of calves and cowherd—boys and thus kept up many Forms for one whole year (X.xiii).

With regard to Bhagavān Śrī Rāma we find it recorded that when the Lord returned to Ayodhyā after the conquest of Laṅkā and the completion of fourteen years of exile, finding the citizens extremely anxious to meet Him, He assumed an infinite number Forms and in a moment met all the people together *(Rāma-caritamānasa, Uttar* V. 3-4).†

This cannot be said to be anything very extraordinary for God. He who holds this entire Universe on His mere thought, who though being One has become many out of mere sport, if the

---

* भगवांस्तदभिप्रेत्य द्वयोः प्रियचिकीर्षया ।
उभयोराविशद्गेहमुभाभ्यां तदलक्षितः ॥
(Bhāgavata X.ixxxvi.26)

† प्रेमातुर सब लोग निहारी। कौतुक कीन्ह कृपाल खरारी ॥
अमित रूप प्रगटे तेहि काला। जथा जोग मिले सबहि कृपाला ॥
छन महिं सबहि मिले भगवाना। उमा मरम यह काहुँ न जाना ॥

same Lord assumes, as in these examples, more than one Form at one and the same time, there is nothing to wonder at it. Even a Yogī can create this miracle. Then, where lies the difficulty for God, who is the Lord of even the Masters of Yoga and the Ruler of Māyā, to do it ?

Now, another question arises—Does God come down to earth under the force of Karma, as we ordinary beings do, when we take our birth ? Is His body also like our bodies a creation of Māyā, and formed of the five elements ? The answer to this question is that in the case of a divine incarnation not a single of these conditions applies. His descent is neither subject to Karma, nor is His Body formed of the five elements, a creation of Māyā. His birth and Karma both are divine and supernatural. His descent is not subject to Karma, because He is wholly beyond Kāla (Time) and Karma. The workings of Karma take place within the jurisdiction of Māyā, while He is wholly beyond Māyā. Therefore, Karma cannot even touch Him. He Himself says in the *Gītā:—*

न मां कर्माणि लिम्पन्ति न मे कर्मफले स्पृहा।
इति मां योऽभिजानाति कर्मभिर्न स बध्यते ॥

(IV. 14)

"I have no desire for the fruit of actions, therefore actions do not affect Me. He who thus knows Me in reality, he, too, is not bound by actions."

Now, when even a person who knows God in reality does not come under the bondage of Karma, it is quite out of the question to raise any discussion about God's birth under the subjection of Karma. God takes a body out of His free-will to confer His grace on His devotees. We may properly understand this from the illustration of a prison. In a prison there live the prisoners and, occasionally, even the owner of the prison, the king himself, goes there for inspection, to confer his grace on the prisoners and also to liberate them from the prison. But there is a world of difference between the king's entering the prison and the prisoners' entering it. The prisoner goes there for undergoing punishment according to royal orders. He is compelled to remain there till the completion of the term of imprisonment, and does not stay there of his own accord. But the king goes there out of his free-will and not for undergoing punishment, and stays there as long as he desires to stay. In the same way God also takes birth, controlling Prakṛti, out of His free-will, and on completion of the Līlā (sport) returns to his Abode without any challenge from any quarter.

When God assumes an incarnation, His Form also is not a Mayic Form like our bodies composed of the five elements, but is wholly Cit (Spirit) in essence, the embodiment of Existence, Knowledge and Bliss. It is a Divine Form, not subject to disease and deterioration. The other point to be noted in this connection is that the birth of the Divine is not similar to the birth of ordinary mortals. A careful reading and reflection on the portion of the *Bhāgavata,* which describes Bhagavān Śrī Kṛṣṇa's manifestation in prison before Vasudeva and Devakī, will make it clear that His birth was not like the birth of ordinary human beings. The unmanifest Paramātmā, the consolidated Form of Existence, Knowledge and Bliss, out of His sport, appeared there in the Form of Viṣṇu, with His emblems, the conch, discus, mace and lotus in four hands. His manifestation and disappearance are part of His independent sports and are not like our births and deaths. Leaving aside God, who is all-powerful, even a Yogī can disappear by his power of Yoga and re-appear in that very form, and in his state of disappearance no one considers him to be dead. When Maharṣi Patañjali and other Masters of Yoga describe such to be the power of a Yogī, then what can be the wonder for God, the Supreme Soul, to disappear and re-appear at will. It is true that Bhagavān Śrī Kṛṣṇa's descent appeared in the eye of ordinary people to be similar to a human birth; but really speaking, it was no birth, it was only His manifestation. That is why on the prayer of mother Devakī, He concealed His four arms and assumed the form of a two-armed child.*

---

* इत्युक्त्वाऽऽसीद्धरिस्तूष्णीं भगवानात्ममायया।
पित्रोः संपश्यतोः सद्यो बभूव प्राकृतः शिशुः॥

(*Bhāgavata* X.iii.46)

"Saying this the Lord stopped, and before the very eyes of His parents quickly assumed, through His own Māyā, the form of an ordinary human child."

In the eleventh chapter of the *Gītā* also, there is a description that on the prayer of Arjuna, Bhagavān Śrī Kṛṣṇa first showed Arjuna His Universal Form, then on another prayer from Arjuna assumed the four-armed Form, and in the end adopted the two-armed human form.

Similarly, with reference to Bhagavān Śrī Rāma, the *Mānasa* describes His manifestation before mother Kausalyā in the four-armed Form, which was subsequently changed on the mother's request into the child-form with two arms. This proves that according to the desire of the devotee, God manifests Himself before the devotee, and granting the latter His auspicious sight, disappears.

It should not be imagined that the Divine Form of God suffers death like the death of the human body. The body that suffers death is left here on earth, but the four-armed Form manifested before Devakī and the Universal Form and four-armed Form manifested before Arjuna, when they disappeared left no trace of them on earth. Not only so, the body through which Bhagavān Śrī Kṛṣṇa carried on all his various activities for the good of the world was also not found in the end. In that Divine Body, He ascended His Supreme Abode, and even after His ascension whenever His Bhaktas earnestly sought Him, He re-appeared before them in that very beautiful Blue-Form and blessed them with His sight and even now blesses them. If His body had really suffered death and dissolution, then how could it be possible for Him to re-appear like this (after his ascent to the Supreme Abode).

This proves that God's ascension to His Supreme Abode is only a disappearance of His Form from earth, and not destruction like that of the perishable human body. The *Bhāgavata* records:—

लोकाभिरामां स्वतनुं धारणाध्यानमङ्गलम् ।
योगधारणयाऽऽग्नेय्यादग्ध्वा धामाविशत्स्वकम् ॥

(XI. xxxi. 6)

"The Lord entered His Supreme Abode without reducing to

ashes by the fire of Yoga His pleasing, enchanting Form, which is most auspicious for the practice of Yogic concentration and meditation."

With reference to Bhagavān Śrī Rāma, the Rāmāyaṇa of Vālmīki says that at the time of the Lord's departure to His Supreme Abode, the Demiurge, Brahmā, together with all Devas came to the bank of the Sarayū and prayed to the Lord to enter His Vaiṣṇava-Body and the Lord, assenting to their prayers, together with the three brothers, entered the manifested body into the Vaiṣṇava-Body.*

That the Divine Body is not a product of Māyā is proved also by the fact that even saints, who delight only in the Self, and are wholly freed from the bondage of Māyā get enchanted and lose all consciousness of the body when they see that incomparable Form which fascinates the three worlds. Had that Form been a creation of Māyā, a modification of the three Guṇas, how could it so strongly move the self-realized Munis, whose desires are all fulfilled, and who live wholly above the plane of the Guṇas ?

When the great patriarch Bhīṣma, awaiting death on his bed of arrows in the battlefield, learnt that Śrī Kṛṣṇa had come to see him, he first of all meditated on the Form of the Lord which fascinates the three worlds, and offered a prayer that he might develop motiveless love for Śrī Kṛṣṇa.† If that Form was a Form of Māyā,

---

* अथ तस्मिन् मुहूर्ते तु ब्रह्मा लोकपितामहः।
सर्वैः परिवृतो देवैर्ऋषिभिश्च महात्मभिः॥
ततः पितामहो वाणीं त्वन्तरिक्षादभाषत।
आगच्छ विष्णो भद्रं ते दिष्ट्या प्राप्तोऽसि राघव॥
भ्रातृभिः सह देवाभैः प्रविशस्व स्विकां तनुम्।
पितामहवचः श्रुत्वा विनिश्चित्य महामतिः।
विवेश वैष्णवं तेजः सशरीरः सहानुजः॥
(*V.R. Uttar.* 110.3,8,9,12)

† त्रिभुवनकमनं तमालवर्णं
रविकरगौरवराम्बरं दधाने।
वपुरलककुलावृताननाब्जं
विजयसखे रतिरस्तु मेऽनवद्या॥
(*Bhāgavata* I. IX.33)

"Let my heart develop disinterested love for Śrī Kṛṣṇa, the friend of Arjuna,

why should a man of wisdom a saintly soul like Bhīṣma, who had withdrawn his faculties from all sides and lived a life of supreme dispassion throughout his career, fix his mind on that Form at the time of death ?

Again, when Śrī Rāma and Lakṣmaṇa, led by Maharṣi Viśvāmitra, went to Janakapur to see the great Bow Sacrifice, what became the condition of Janaka, the chief of Jñānīs, (man of knowledge) at the sight of the incomparable pair of brothers ? Gosvāmī Tulasīdāsajī has most graphically described this condition in beautiful language, which we quote below:—

मूरति मधुर मनोहर देखी। भयउ बिदेहु बिदेहु बिसेषी॥
प्रेम मगन मनु जानि नृपु करि बिबेकु धरि धीर।
बोलेउ मुनि पद नाइ सिरु गदगद गिरा गभीर॥
सहज बिरागरूप मनु मोरा। थकित होत जिमि चंद चकोरा॥
इन्हहि बिलोकत अति अनुरागा। बरबस ब्रह्मसुखहि मन त्यागा॥
पुनि पुनि प्रभुहि चितव नरनाहू। पुलक गात उर अधिक उछाहू॥

(Mānasa Bālakāṇḍa)

"Seeing the sweet, enchanting Form, Videha (Janaka) became all the more Videha (devoid of body consciousness). Finding that his heart is merged in love, the king steadied himself through his discrimination. Bowing his head at the feet of the sage he said in a choked voice deep with emotion. 'O Lord, my mind, which is by nature full of dispassion, gets enchanted by their sight as the Cakora gets enchanted by the sight of the moon. As soon as they came to my sight my mind got overwhelmed with extreme love, and has renounced, as if by force, the Bliss of Brahma.' The king gazed and gazed at the Lord, his body marked by horripilation and the heart full of delight."

The above discussion makes it clear that the Form of the

who fascinates the three worlds by His Beauty, who possesses a blue colour like that of the Tamāla tree, who wears a yellow robe as bright as the rays of the Sun and over whose lotus-like face flows curls of hair."

Avatāra is not a product of Māyā, that the birth and Karma of Avatāras are supernatural—"My birth and activities are Divine" (*Gītā* IV.9), and that those Forms of God manifest themselves out of God's free will and not being subject to Karma, drawn by the love of devotees and in order to bless them with Divine grace. Now, we shall examine what are the scriptures which uphold and establish the manifestation of the Divine in the Form of His incarnations. We have already quoted the *Śrīmad Bhāgavata, Gītā, Vālmīki Rāmāyaṇa* and the *Rāmāyaṇa* of Gosvāmī Tulasīdāsa as our authorities, and shall now show that the *Upaniṣad,* the *Mahābhārata* and other books also prove the descent of God.

The *Kenopaniṣad* records a beautiful illustration. On a certain occasion God helped the Devas and brought victory to them in their fight against the Asuras. The Devas were swollen by pride over this victory. They thought they gained the victory by their own unaided efforts. This is the mental defect from which all Jīvas suffer. Although the real doer is God Himself, owing to the ego the Jīva feels himself to be the doer and gets entangled in the net of bondage. But God is omniscient as well as the humbler of pride. He came to know the obsession from which the Devas suffered, and in order to remove their pride He manifested Himself before them in the strange Form of a Yakṣa (Demigod). Enchanted by Māyā, the Devas did not know who the Yakṣa was. If God desires to conceal His identity there is none who possesses the power to penetrate His mystery. He can be known only by those to whom out of grace He reveals His identity and not others—'He alone comes to know You, to whom You make Yourself known.' That Arch-Magician has so artfully concealed Himself under the screen of Māyā that it is not possible for anybody easily to recognize Him. The Lord Himself says in the *Gītā*:—

नाहं प्रकाशः सर्वस्य योगमायासमावृतः ।

(VII.25)

"Veiled by My Yogamāyā, I am not manifest to all."

The chief of Devas, Indra, sent one after another, the god of Fire, and the god of Air to find out who the Yakṣa was. In order to show them that all the world functioned through the strength supplied by Him, that whatever power the Devas possessed were but gifts from Him, that without His help not even a small leaf could move, Brahma placed a blade of grass before the god of Fire and asked him to burn it. The Fire-god, who cherished the pride of being able to burn the entire universe, applied all his strength, but could not burn that small blade of grass, and overwhelmed by a sense of shame quietly returned from the interview. Then, came the turn of the god of Air. He was obsessed by the pride of being able to blow away all objects on earth, but he also failed to move that single blade of grass. How could he move it ? All his powers had been taken over by Brahma, who was the source of those powers. Deprived of his powers, what was left in him on the strength of which he could act ? What to talk of the strength of God, the powers of Devas like the Fire-god, etc., get dulled even in the presence of devotees of God. There was an occasion when even before the great devotee Prahlāda, the power of Fire-god proved futile and he became as cold as water—'पावकोऽपि सलिलायतेऽधुना।' In the case of Bhakta Sudhanvā, boiling oil in a cauldron placed on fire failed to burn him.

Lastly, the chief of gods, Indra himself, went to the Yakṣa, but seeing him the Yakṣa disappeared. Immediately after this Haimavatī Umādevī (Pārvatī) appeared on the scene, and She informed Indra that the manifestation which disappeared from before him was Brahma Himself. This information opened Indra's eyes and he realized that God enacted this sport in order only to humble the pride of the Devas *(Kenopaniṣad* III).

Thus the *Upaniṣads* also contain reference to the appearance of Brahma through the assumption of a Form; and it is not the *Purāṇas* alone that mention God as manifesting Himself through Forms. Over and above the *Gītā,* the *Mahābhārata* contains other illustrations which go to support the theory of God's incarnation on earth. As the space at our disposal is short we shall satisfy ourselves by mentioning only one such instance. On the conclusion of the *Mahābhārata* war when Bhagavān Śrī Kṛṣṇa was returning to Dvārakā, He met the illustrious sage Uttaṅka on His way. In the course of their conversation when the Muni learnt that Śrī Kṛṣṇa had failed to bring about peace between the Kauravas and Pāṇḍavas eventually resulting in a terrible battle between the two parties in which all Kauravas had been slain, he got extremely angry with Śrī Kṛṣṇa. He said—'O Kṛṣṇa, the Kauravas were Your relations; had You but wished it, You could stop this war and thus save them. But though possessed of power, You did not save them. I shall, therefore, curse You.' Having heard these angry words of the Muni, Śrī Kṛṣṇa smiled within Himself and replied, 'O Muni, no one can overpower Me with his penance. I do not want that all your Tapas should be uselessly destroyed. Therefore, know Me, first who I am, and then decide about cursing Me.' Saying this, the Lord started to describe His glory to the Muni. He said, 'O prince among Munis, I am the resting place of the three Guṇas—Sattva, Raja and Tama, and know Rudra and the Vasus also to have born out of Me. Know this for certain that all beings in creation are within Me, and I am within all beings. The Daityas, snakes, Gandharvas, Rākṣasas, Nāgas and Apsarās all emanate from Me. What people call being and non-being, manifest and non-manifest, perishable and imperishable—all these are My Forms. The Dharma of the four Āśramas and Vedic rituals are also my Forms. The Veda which begins with Oṁ, articles of offering in the sacrifice, the priests offering sacrifice know all these to be Myself alone. The Sāma-chanters praise Me through their chants; in ceremonies of expiation, the priests who chant propitiatory verses praise Me alone. I incarnate Myself in various species of beings for the protection and establishment of Dharma. I am Viṣṇu, I am Brahmā, I am the origin and I am the dissolution. I alone am the creator and destroyer of all beings. Whenever ages change, I take birth with the motive of doing good to all and establish the reign of righteousness. When I take birth among Devas, I behave like Devas, when I incarnate Myself among Gandharvas I behave like Gandharvas; when I appear among Nāgas I begin to act like Nāgas; and when I enter Yakṣa and other species, I behave according to those very species. Now, I have appeared among men, therefore I am behaving like a human being. Approaching the Kauravas, I tried My very best to induce them to establish peace; but possessed by delusion, they rejected all My proposals. I tried to bring them round even by threat; but overcome, as they were by vice and caught in the jaws of Death, they could not be brought round. Consequently, they all perished in the battle' Hearing these words of the Lord, the eyes of the Muni were opened. Then, on the entreaty of the Muni, the Lord showed him the Universal Form—the form which was revealed before Arjuna (*Mahābhārata* Aśvamedha Parva, chap. 53—55).

The above statement also thoroughly establishes the theory of Avatārahood. It proves, too, that God appears as Avatāra not only among men, but in other species of beings as well. For all the species are His and it is He alone who is sporting through the various forms of beings. God's incarnations as Fish (Matsya), Tortoise (Kūrma), Boar (Varāha), Man-Lion (Nṛsiṅgha) and Dwarf (Vāmana) the descriptions of which are found in the *Purāṇas,* were such incarnations. The article would be inordinately long if we take up all these Avatāras for discussion. Therefore, we had to confine ourselves for the present primarily with facts relating to the two most prominent incarnations, Bhagavān Śrī Rāma and Bhagavān Śrī Kṛṣṇa.

Over and above these, there is another Form of God's incarnation known as Arcāvatāra, or God's descent for worship by the devotee. Images of God made of metal, stone and earth, etc., are called God's Arcā Vigraha (Forms for worship). Through the power of Love and faith of the devotee, these Images occasionally become living and begin to move, smile and speak. The descent of the power of God on these Images is called Arcāvatāra. From the records of the lives of many devotees, we come to know that the images of the Deity they worshipped used to behave with them as possessed of life. Through the cultivation of devotion to God by taking shelter under any of these incarnations one may, through His grace, easily gain strong attachment to God's feet and thereby attain salvation. This is the supreme goal of human existence.

All the Ācāryas of the different Dualistic schools of philosophy have recognized the theory of Avatāra in their schemes of thought. Among them some schools worship the Form of Bhagavān Śrī Rāma and others worship the Form of Bhagavān Śrī Kṛṣṇa as the Supreme Deity. The great Ācārya of the Advaita school Svāmī Śaṅkarācārya also in the introduction to his commentary on the *Gītā* recognized Bhagavān Śrī Kṛṣṇa as an incarnation of the Primal Being, Bhagavān Nārāyana. He says:—

दीर्घेण कालेन अनुष्ठातॄणां कामोद्भवाद् हीयमानविवेक-विज्ञानहेतुकेन अधर्मेण अभिभूयमाने धर्मे प्रवर्धमाने च अधर्मे, जगतः स्थितिं परिपिपालयिषुः स आदिकर्ता नारायणाख्यो विष्णुः—भौमस्य ब्रह्मणो ब्राह्मणत्वस्य रक्षणार्थं देवक्यां वसुदेवाद् अंशेन कृष्णः किल सम्बभूव। ब्राह्मणत्वस्य हि रक्षणेन रक्षितः स्याद् वैदिको धर्मस्तदधीनत्वाद् वर्णाश्रमभेदानाम्। स च भगवान् ज्ञानैश्वर्यशक्तिबलवीर्यतेजोभिः सदा सम्पन्नस्त्रिगुणात्मिकां वैष्णवीं स्वां मायां मूलप्रकृतिं वशीकृत्य अजः अव्ययो भूतानामीश्वरो नित्यशुद्धबुद्धमुक्तस्वभावऽपि सन् स्वमायया देहवानिव जात इव च लोकानुग्रहं कुर्वनिव लक्ष्यते।

"When the light of knowledge and discrimination in people who have been observing the practices of religion for long gets darkened through growth of worldly desires, which states the çause of His manifestation, when righteousness began to be overcome by unrighteousness and evil began to predominate, then Bhagavān Viṣṇu, who is known also as Nārāyaṇa, the Primal Being, who is interested in the preservation of creation, manifested Himself in the form of Śrī Kṛṣṇa through Devakī and Vasudeva for the protection of the representatives of Brahma on earth, that is, the Brāhmaṇas and their Brahmanhood.

Through the protection of Brahmanhood alone Vedic Dharma will be properly protected. For, the divisions of Varṇāśrama depend on it.

That Lord, possessed of the complete attributes of God viz., knowledge, splendour, power, might, energy and glory etc., although unborn and imperishable, master and lord of all creation, eternally pure, awakened and free in character yet controlling His Vaiṣṇavī Māyā, which is the primordial Prakṛti consisting of three Guṇas, appears through His sport as having been born like ordinary mortals and showering His grace on them."

Through many such arguments, the Ācārya established the divinity of Bhagavān Śrī Kṛṣṇa and His identity with the Brahma of Vedānta. Bowing, again and again, to that supremely compassionate Lord, Bhagavān Śrī Kṛṣṇa, we shall close the article with our final observations. Those who feel themselves wholly incapable of realizing God by their own unaided efforts, who look constantly to the descent of the Lord's grace and depend entirely on Him as a baby depends on the mother, make the Lord extremely eager to meet them, who actually runs to meet them as does the mother cow to meet her new born calf. Therefore let us all take refuge in the most merciful Lord, and in order to rouse His compassion on us, let us try to devote ourselves to the best of our ability to the constant practices of His Bhajana and meditation with full faith, reverence and devotion.

The Longing for God-Vision

Many a friend complain that although they may try their best, God does not favour them with His vision. They describe God as 'cruel', 'hard-hearted', and imagine that the Lord's heart is as hard as adamant and never melts. What interest has He in taking care of us, in granting us His vision, or making us His own ? These and similar charges they level against God.

The fact, however, is quite the reverse of it. The Lord's mercy on us is unlimited. He eagerly awaits every opportunity to manifest Himself and tries on every occasion to bless the devotee with His vision. He helps us at every step in all our spiritual effort. It is a common experience in the world that one has to hasten to a place where his affections are centred. He who has special attraction for us compels us to go to him leaving all engagements aside. When one refrains from going to a place, it indicates that love is deficient there. When such is the case with ordinary men like us, where is to wonder that God, who is an ocean of Love and compassion, should be ready to grant us Divine vision, if we possess only a little love for Him ?

The main reason for delay in the Lord's manifestation is our want of attraction for Him. He is the very embodiment of Love and Grace. How can He Himself delay in appearing before us ? The reason therefore is clear. We lack the qualification to gain His vision. We are markedly deficient in faith and Love. In order to increase our faith and Love, we should try to the best of our ability to gain the knowledge of His truth, secret, virtues and power. It is never possible that the Lord will not meet a devotee even after the latter has gained faith and Love. He becomes compelled, then, to bring the devotee's faith to fruition. How can we hope to gain the Lord's favour till we have developed complete faith in His Grace ? If we come to believe that God-vision can be actually gained, and that a certain person has gained the vision, we cannot even guess the depth of attraction we shall exhibit in our behaviour towards him. It is quite impossible to imagine what will be the condition when one actually comes face to face with God Himself.

What was the state of the Gopīs when the Lord disappeared from their midst at the time of the Rāsa-dance ? Separation from the Lord became unbearable to them even for a moment, therefore the Lord was compelled to manifest Himself before them. When Durvāsā, with ten thousand disciples, came and asked for food at an untimely hour, Draupadī finding no means to entertain the guests began anxiously to remember God. The Lord manifested Himself as soon as she uttered her cry of distress, as if He was already present there. Almost all devotees, when they develop faith gain this experience. Narasī Mehatā had an unshakable faith that the Lord would come with presents to help in the marriage ceremony of his daughter, therefore absorbed in devotion he began to sing "O child, He will come, He will come, He will come; I have complete faith that the Lord will come." He had not the least doubt about the Lord's coming. Therefore, the Lord was compelled to appear at the proper time.

The only reason for the delay in God-vision is lack of faith. By whatever means the mental resolution is formed, once it is formed, it is impossible that God would refuse to come. He is by nature incapable of disappointing the devotee. If now and then obstacles appear before us and our mind gets perturbed thereby, that is a different matter. But if the devotee refuses to lose his balance of mind during those trials and clings to the Lord with all his might, and declines like Prahlāda to be overcome by the obstacles, he is sure to gain his desired object. The Lord deals with us, now harshly, and now softly, only with as view to strengthen our faith.

Truly speaking faith has such inherent strength that it compels God to manifest Himself in order to bring it to fruition. If the philosopher's stone is a genuine stone, and the iron is pure iron, their contact is bound to transform the iron into gold. The Lord brings success to the faithful devotee by removing all his deficiencies. When faith is properly developed, the deficiencies are automatically removed by the grace of God. It is clear that we lack faith and Love, that is why God does not manifest Himself before us. If not so, looking to His compassionate and loving nature, it appears impossible that the Lord should rest without granting us His sight. When Rāvaṇa forcibly took away Sītā, Śrī Rāma got so much distressed over the incident that there was nothing to distinguish Him from an ordinary man of the world devoted to his wife. What was the reason for this ? The reason was that Sītā could not live without Rāma even for a moment. The Lord says, 'In whatever way men worship Me, in the same way do I seek them.'

ये यथा मां प्रपद्यन्ते तांस्तथैव भजाम्यहम्।

(*Gītā* IV.11)

The Lord is ever ready to manifest Himself. He, as if, longs that people should love Him so that He might appear before them. If we can develop the intensity of Love which Sītā bore to Bhagavān Śrī Rāmacandra, we shall find the Lord ever ready for us. He who longs for the Lord, the Lord longs for him in the same manner and to the same extent.

That our faith and Love for the Lord may grow from more to more, that our remembrance of Him may remain constant, that we may not forget Him even for the wink of an eye, should ever remain our goal. Let Him keep us in whatever state He likes, in whatever place He likes, but let His remembrance ever remain unbroken and constant with us. Let us feel pleasure in His pleasure and happy in His happiness. If the Lord desires to keep us in hell, we should not cast even a look at Vaikuṇṭha, His own abode, and should feel the greatest pleasure in living in hell. When one completely surrenders oneself to the Lord, he can no longer desire or seek anything from the Lord. When the Lord becomes ours, and we become His, what else should remain to be accomplished by us ? We are so many children of the Lord. The mother does not care for the defects of her child. Her heart ever remains full of affection for the child. If the Lord begins to examine our deficiencies, we shall be nowhere. He is ever anxious for an opportunity that He may manifest Himself before us. But we ourselves become obstacles in the way of His manifestation. This may not appear from external show; in fact, we may give the impression that we are longing for His sight. But where is that sincere longing of the heart ? We may not actually utter the words, "Not now, Lord, wait still awhile," but our actions clearly say so. The very fact of being able to bear delay in the Lord's manifestation constitutes our asking Him to wait. We are separated from the Lord, because we do not feel sufficiently perturbed over that separation. When we ourselves are prepared to bear the separation, when owing to this separation there is no agitation, no sorrow in our heart, why should the Lord care for us ? There would have been some point in the complaint, if there had been real agitation in us and yet the Lord failed to appear. With pleasure we are alive without Him. And yet if He does not appear before us, wherein lies His fault ? He is, indeed, ever ready to manifest Himself, but till there is craving in us, how can He appear ? The first requisite of God-vision is intense thirst for such vision. The Lord alone knows what should be the character of that thirst. The thirst which compels the Lord to manifest Himself should be regarded as the proper thirst. Therefore, one should go on increasing this thirst till the Lord actually appears before him. When the vessel will get filled, water will overflow automatically.

The state of Divine Love is a wonderful state. When a talk about God is proceeding and both the speaker and his hearers are absorbed in tasting the sweet nectar of that talk, let it proceed even if God Himself appears on the scene, let it not by any means be disturbed. There is a peculiar sweet taste in all talks of the dearest. When one develops relish for it, he will not desire anything else. The ways of Love are quite peculiar and uncommon. He who has got the relish of Divine Love, what else requires to be accomplished by him ? The Lord examines only one's Love. And Divine Love stands on a higher pedestal than even the Lord Himself. Absorption in Lord's meditation with faith and devotion, with consciousness about the Lord's virtues, power, truth and secrets, means tasting of Divine Love, or being plunged in the Divine essence.

If two lovers take the vow of silence as between themselves, the one whose love is greater will lose in the contest. If the husband and wife start a competition of not speaking with one another, the one whose affection is greater will lose. In the same way, when there is a competition between the devotee and God, the Lord has to accept defeat, for there is none whose love is greater than His. Such an agitation should be created in Him that He cannot stay without us even for a moment. Then He will be bound to accept defeat, and will be compelled to appear before us. Such is the condition we should create; we should fascinate Him by our love. Then He will not leave us even if we may try to drive Him out by force.

Our attitude towards the Lord should be like the attitude of a wife towards her husband. Just as the wife fascinates her husband by her love and sweet behaviour, even so we should try to fascinate the Lord. Let us without indulging in any flattery make Him feel attracted towards us. He will not then leave our door even for the wink of an eye. A beggar of Love, He will be in the bondage of Love. Where can He go leaving us in the lurch ? How can a husband ignore the love of a devoted wife ? Even so, how can the Lord be indifferent to the Love of a devotee ? When we develop this attitude, He will never be able to stay anywhere without us ? He is always bound by His Love. Let us once bind Him by Love, He will then ever remain bound to us.

We should learn from a woman the art of capturing the Lord. We should cultivate with Him the relation as between a man and his wife. This is cultivation of the sweet sentiment. There is no necessity to change one's dress, but let us be creatures of the Lord through internal sentiment. This is the best way of realizing Him.

The Lord is extremely kind and generous. Therefore, He may be realized if one cultivates only a slight degree of Love for Him, but let us proceed with the Love as depicted above as our goal. For Divine Love can be attained if we proceed aiming at a goal which is sufficiently high. If, according to that goal, we succeed in gaining full Divine Love, it would be a matter of great fortune with us. Such a person will be regarded as an ideal before the world, a sanctifying object of sight. A glance from his eyes will bring spiritual awakening in others; then what more need be said personally about his own self ?

Dialogue with the Lord during Meditation

Let the Sādhaka retire to a solitary place and take his seat in yogic posture like the Svastika, Siddha or the Lotus posture, on a seat made either of the holy Kuśa grass or of wool, keeping his spine erect, and without feeling any inconvenience. Let him then withdraw his senses from their respective objects and renouncing all worldly thoughts make the mind totally void of impressions. Thereafter let him invoke the Lord, the Deity of his heart, in a pure state of mind, free of sloth and full of dispassion. He should know that when the Lord will appear before him during meditation, the mind will be full of joy, peace and light and although his eyes may remain closed he will, as if, see the whole universe lighted up by a supernatural light. Where there is peace there will be no distraction, and where the light of knowledge shines there will be no sleep or sloth. He should firmly believe that when God is invoked and prayers are offered to Him, the Lord appears before the devotee during meditation. There should be no difficulty in meditating on the Form of one's own Deity. The question may be raised that when it is easy to meditate on a Form which one has actually seen, is it ever possible to meditate on a Form which has not been seen ? The answer to this is that meditation on a Divine Form is possible by reading the description of a Form in the scriptures or hearing the same from the lips of saints, or selecting a picture of the Deity which appeals to one's heart. Therefore, the Sādhaka should invoke the Deity by closing his eyes. If such invocation fails to bring the Lord, let him loudly chant His Names and virtues, offer Him prayers and hymns and go on repeating the invocation with full faith and Love in a voice choked with emotion. Full of hope that the Lord will come, and expectant of His arrival, let the devotee chant the hymn:—

एक बात मैं पूछहु तोही। कारन कवन बिसारेहु मोही ॥

"(O Lord) one word I ask Thee. Why hast Thou forgotten me."

Let him, then, believe that the Lord has appeared before him, and stands in the air at a distance of about two feet from him. Carefully observing every part of that Divine Form, from feet to head, let him chant:—

नाथ सकल साधनकर हीना। कीन्ही कृपा जानि जन दीना ॥

"O Lord, though I am deficient in every form of spiritual discipline, Thou hast shown me Your grace, knowing me to be poor in spirit."

'O Lord, I have no spiritual practice to my credit, and yet You have shown me Your favour finding me poor and helpless. I possess nothing on the strength of which I can claim Your vision even in meditation. But You have granted me this vision knowing me to be humble in spirit.'

Thus on the appearance of the Lord during meditation, the Sādhaka will start conversation with Him.

Sādhaka:—O Lord, why do You take such a long time to appear even at the time of meditation ? Why do You not come the moment You are sought ? Why do You keep one longing for such a length of time.

Lord:—In keeping you longing lies your greatest good.

S:—I do not understand what good lies in the longing. I think good lies only in Your Appearance.

L:—A special object is gained by the delay in My Appearance. The separation is then intensely felt, and the desire for union is accentuated. Appearance at that state leads to a special kind of joy. When there is intense hunger, food tastes sweet like nectar.

S:—I agree. But if the appearance is put off indefinitely, the Sādhaka, being hopeless, may give up his meditation.

L:—If faith in Me is so weak that delay in My Appearance may tire out the Sādhaka and cause him give up meditation, what purpose will be served by My Appearing before him ?

S:—Your Appearance will increase his taste in You. That will make him intensify his spiritual efforts. Therefore, it seems to me proper that You should appear the moment a Sādhaka calls out for You.

L:—The propriety of a thing is determined by what I Myself consider to be proper, and I do only that which is proper.

S:—O Lord, I should certainly admit whatever You say, but the mind is exceptionally base. It prevents me from accepting it. What You say is no doubt the truth, and yet I like that You should appear the moment I call You. Please tell me what is the nature of that cry which, when uttered even once, compels You to appear.

L:—I may appear like that when a Sādhaka gets agitated on account of My separation even as the Gopīs got agitated, or when he cries out through distress even as Draupadī and Gajendra did with Love and faith in Me. Or, I may appear even unasked before a devotee, who, like Prahlāda, practises devotion without any interested motive.

S:—Why do You appear after making the devotee feel intensely agitated over Your separation ? Why do You make him pass through the agony of separation ?

L:—The agony of separation has a very high place in the realm of spiritual experience. It intensifies Divine Love. The devotee who experiences this agony finds it difficult to live without Me even for a moment. Thus he attains Me for all time. He never loses hold of Me after once realizing Me. Bharata had suffered the agony of separation for fourteen long years, but thereafter he was never separated from Me.

S:—Whenever You required anything to be done, You entrusted either Lakṣmaṇa or Śatrughna to do it, and not Bharata. What was the secret of it ?

L:—Owing to excess of Love, Bharata could not bear separation from me.

S:—Then, how had he borne it for fourteen years ?

L:—He had to bear it under my order, but this separation intensified his Love so greatly that thereafter he had never to suffer separation from Me.

S:—When ordaining that long separation, what was the special good You intended for Bharata ?

L:—Through the experience of separation for fourteen years, he learnt the true secret of separation and union. Then, he began to feel even a moment's separation as long in duration as that of an age. Without that, how could he develop this intense attraction for Me ?

S:—The pain of separation may develop despair well as in a Sādhaka.

L:—I have already said that it is useless for Me to appear before such a Sādhaka.

S:—Then, what should such a Sādhaka do to gain the privilege of Your sight ?

L:—He should try his utmost to increase Love and Faith in Me.

S:—Is it, then, wholly impossible to gain Your vision without Faith and Love ?

L:—Yes, it is wholly impossible. This is the wisest rule.

S:—Can You not make an exception to this rule ?

L:—If I make an exception in favour of one, and refuse to do it with regard to another, I shall be guilty of partiality of conduct. Exception to the rule cannot be made with regard to all.

S:—Is there any circumstance when this rule is not applied ?

L:—Yes, there is. This rule is not applied when a person departs from this world. At that time mere remembrance of Me, whether with or without Faith and Love, will lead to My realization.

S:—Why is this special exception made with regard to the departing soul ?

L:—His life is then coming to its end. He is leaving the human body for an indefinite period of time. That is why at that moment the rule is specially kept in abeyance with reference to him.

S:—It is quite in the fitness of things that this special exception should be made with regard to the departing soul. But at the time of death control over the mind, intellect and senses are lost; therefore it may not be within the power of man to remember You at that critical moment.

L:—For that purpose the habit of constant remembrance of Me should be formed. He who cultivates this habit will certainly remember Me at the last moment.

S:—I have a desire that I may maintain constant remembrance of You, and I try also to maintain it, but the fickle and wayward mind does not allow me to do so. What should I do under the circumstance ?

L:—Withdraw the mind from every object which may tempt it; argue with it as you would do with a loving friend, and try, again and again, to fix it on Me. Or, knowing Me to be present in every object, meditate on Me in the very object which may tempt it.

S:—I heard this advice from others also, have read about it and understand its efficacy. But I forget it when the mind begins to wander like an unbroken horse. That is why I fail to maintain constant remembrance of You.

L:—You are subject to this bad habit because of your worldly attachments. For removal of these attachments and rectification of the habit you should cultivate association with saints (Satsaṅga) and practise Japa of the Divine Name.

S:—Both these are done by me to a certain extent, and I recognize their efficacy, but such is my misfortune that I cannot continue them for all the time.

L:—Where lies your misfortune in this ? Your failure in these matters shows nothing but deficiency of effort on your part.

S:—O Lord, are the practices of Bhajana and Satsaṅga subject to effort ? I have heard that Satsaṅga is possible only when there is an accumulation of one's past merits.

L:—When a Sādhaka makes effort for the practice of Bhajana, subordinating himself either to Me or to a saint, it will certainly bring him success. Evil association, worldly attachments and stored up latencies of past Karma no doubt hinder his progress, but these obstacles are removed through the intense practice of Bhajana. Then his progress will be steady and Faith and Love will increase. Obstacles will cease to exist for him. Prārabdha, or the Karma which has begun to bear fruit, brings him only joy or sorrow according to his past Karma. It cannot frustrate new auspicious deeds. Obstacles appear because of the weakness of the Sādhaka. Apart from past merits, Satsaṅga may be obtained through My grace even through the effort of a Sādhaka, when it is made with reverence and Love.

S:—O Lord, there are men who try to obtain Satsaṅga, but when they fail to obtain it, they begin to denounce their fate. Is this proper for them ?

L:—Well, there is danger of self-deception in this. It may bring slackness in spiritual effort. If after the best of efforts one fails to obtain Satsaṅga, there may be some justification for this; but even then instead of blaming the Prārabdha, the proper course should be to blame the deficiencies in reverence and Love, for through reverence and Love new Prārabdha may be created and bring one the most auspicious gift of Satsaṅga.

S:—O Lord, why do You extol the glory of Satsaṅga so highly ?

L:—Without Satsaṅga practices like Bhajana, meditation and selfless service are not possible, and exclusive Love for Me, cannot be developed. Without it realization of Me is difficult. That is why I extol Satsaṅga so highly.

S:—O Lord, then tell me what should be done to obtain Satsaṅga ?

L:—I have already told you that when one makes an effort with Faith and Love to obtain Satsaṅga, he may obtain it through My grace.

S:—Now, I shall, make further and more determined effort to obtain Satsaṅga. From You also I seek help that I may have constant Bhajana and meditation with a heart full of Love, and without any interested motive.

L:—What you seek is quite right so far as your understanding goes, but your mind does not relish it so well as it does enjoyment of worldly objects.

S:—Yes, Lord, what I seek is from the intellect only, but the mind is a veritable rascal. That is why when it does not relish Bhajana and meditation, I am helpless before it. It is one more reason why You should send me special aid.

L:—If the mind does not relish Bhajana and meditation, even then you should continue to try to fix it in those practices. Gradually it will get the relish, and then proper Bhajana and meditation will be possible.

S:—I have been trying according to my capacity and power, but the result has not yet been quite satisfactory. That is why I feel somewhat disheartened. I have faith that I may succeed through Your grace. That is why I humbly solicit Your grace.

L:—No, you should not lose heart. Everything is possible if the burden is shifted on Me. That is all right, but out of deference to My instruction, you should also put forth your best effort. Never delude yourself into the belief that you have done all that is humanly possible; there is yet a good deal of deficiency in your effort. You have not yet devoted all your strength to it. Therefore, strive and strive with all your heart.

S:—Taking shelter under You, I shall no doubt try again, but, O Lord, success depends only on Your grace.

L:—It is no doubt out of love that you say you depend on Me. But take care that it may not lead you to the error of slackness in effort. I say that you should put more strength into your exertion. When that is my instruction, there is no reason why your exertion should lose its strength. It is only your mind which is playing this deception on you. Never allow the mind to entertain any thought of despair; nourish it always with hope.

S:—When I fail to obtain peace and joy, I begin to lose hope.

L:—When you depend on Me, why do you turn your thought to the success of an effort ? That is also a form of desire.

S:—No doubt it is a desire, but its purpose is to advance Bhajana and meditation.

L:—When you have taken refuge in Me, why do you worry for peace and joy so that your Bhajana and meditation may advance ? You should devote your attention to carrying out My instruction, and not to the fruit of your effort.

S:—Failure in the effort will bring loss of hope, and loss of hope will interfere with Bhajana and meditation.

L:—That is all right, nevertheless there should be no loss of hope because of a certain amount of failure in effort. With faith in Me, and out of deference to My instruction, one should gradually go on increasing his exertion.

S:—This is quite proper and reasonable, and yet, O Lord, when there is no peace and joy, loss of hope is forced on me.

L:—If such is the case, you do not seem to have heard Me with care and attention. You are subject to a deception by the mind.

S:—O Lord, is this not caused by the stored up impressions of my past sins ? Are they not damping my ardour ?

L:—When one surrenders oneself to Me, his sins are all destroyed.

S:—Yes, Lord, I know this; but where is that complete surrender in my case ? I have been making only a lip profession of surrender to You.

L:—I do not abandon even one who makes a lip profession of surrender to Me. But you should try to the best of your ability to surrender yourself in consonance with the sentiment of your heart.

S:—I try my best, but the vagaries of the mind make me quite helpless.

L:—It is an error on your part to regard that you are trying your best. As a matter of fact you try very little, but regard it as a large effort.

S:—I shall make special attempt to remedy this defect. But owing to fondness for the body, attachment to objects of worldly enjoyment and fickleness of the mind, it appears to me very hard to succeed in the attempt to complete surrender without the help of Your grace.

L:—You regard it hard, therefore it appears hard. As a matter of fact, it is not so hard.

S:—Why should I not regard it hard ? Through practical experience I find it so.

L:—If that is your experience, let it remain so; but you should fix your attention exclusively on my words.

S:—Depending on Your grace I shall try from now that it may not appear difficult to me. But I have heard that all sins get destroyed through even a slight practice of Japa of Your Name and meditation of Your Form. You Yourself and the scriptures say so; then why are my mental impulses so filthy ? However slight and defective they may be, Bhajana and meditation are performed to a certain extent even by me.

L:—It is true that sins get destroyed through the practices of Bhajana and meditation. But who believes in this ? You also do not possess full faith in this, for you yourself regard that your sins are not destroyed, and they remain as they were before.

S:—What is the cause of this lack of faith ?

L:—Association with persons who are vile* and unbelievers,† stored up impressions of sins and evil impulses.

S:—Are sin and evil impulses two different kinds of evil ?

L:—Theft, adultery, falsehood, killing of animals, hypocrisy, etc., are sins; attraction, repulsion, lust, anger, arrogance, egotism, etc., are evil impulses.

S:—How are they to be destroyed ?

L:—The best way of destroying them is to devote oneself disinterestedly to the practices of Bhajana, meditation, selfless service and Satsaṅga, etc.

S:—Some say that when dispassion is developed, evils like

---

* Vile persons are those who indulge in activities prohibited by the scriptures, viz., falsehood, deception, theft, adultery, killing of animals, etc.

† Unbelievers are those who have no faith in God and do not believe in the scriptures like the Śrutis, Smṛtis, etc.

attraction and repulsion get automatically destroyed, and thereafter Bhajana and meditation can be practiced in a satisfactory way.

L:—Yes, it is true that dispassion helps to advance Bhajana and meditation. But without purification of the heart dispassion cannot be firmly established. If you say that dispassion may be developed by cultivation of thoughts of sorrow and evil involved in the body and worldly enjoyments, I agree with it. But these thoughts also develop as the result of the practices enunciated above. Therefore, utmost effort should be made for carrying on the practices of Bhajana, meditation, selfless service and Satsanga.

S:—O Lord, now please tell me when You will grant me Your direct vision.

L:—Why do you worry over this ? I shall do so what time appears quite appropriate to Me. When the time arrives the physician himself prescribes regular diet for the patient. The patient should completely depend on the physician for this.

S:—I admit it. But when the patient feels hungry, he goes on repeating, "When shall I get my regular diet ?" He who is afflicted with a strong hunger cannot but go on asking for food.

L:—The physician knows whether the hunger of the patient is true or false. If he refrains from prescribing food even when the patient feels a strong hunger, the restraint is all for the patient's good.

S:—This is so, I admit; but I do not understand what good may underlie Your withholding divine vision from a Sādhaka. I see good involved only in Your granting him the vision. Inappropriate food may bring harm to a patient but Your vision may never bring any harm; on the contrary, it brings supreme good; therefore, Your realization cannot be compared to the diet of a patient.

L:—The physician prescribes in proper time the diet which he feels will contribute to the gradual recovery of the patient. In this matter the patient has to depend on the judgment of the physician. The physician allows solid food to the patient when he thinks the latter's true hunger is awakened, and this brings no harm to the patient. Though My realization brings supreme good, yet this is not possible without the awakening of true hunger in the form of development of full Love and Faith in Me.

S:—There is great deficiency in me so far as Love and Faith are concerned, and I consider it very hard to remove this defect. Therefore, Your vision is certainly most difficult, if not impossible in my case.

L:—It is an error on your part to hold this view. The vision is delayed because of this view.

S:—What can I do other than hold this view ? Why should I not hold it ? Divine vision is impossible without full Faith and Love, and I find myself wholly deficient in both these respects.

L:—Can this deficiency not be removed ?

S:—It may be; but if the rate of progress is to be measured by what happened in the past, it is not possible for the deficiency to disappear in this life.

L:—Why do you yourself put an obstacle in the way of your progress by holding this view ? Can the work of a hundred years not be accomplished in the course of a minute ?

S:—Yes, everything is possible through Your grace.

L:—Then why did you come to the conclusion that the accomplishment was impossible in this very life ?

S:—This was due to my foolishness, but now please have mercy on me, Lord, that I may soon develop full Faith in an exclusive Love for You.

L:—Do I not want that you should develop this ? Do I put any obstacle in the way of this development ?

S:—There can be no question of putting obstacle in this matter. You are no doubt rendering me the necessary aid and yet there is delay in my removing the deficiencies of Faith and Love. That is why I pray for Your grace.

L:—That is all right. But in order to remove the deficiencies of Faith and Love you should rely on Me and make the best possible effort.

S:—O Lord, I have heard it said that these deficiencies may be removed if one weeps before You. Is this a fact ?

L:—That weeping is a different kind of weeping.

S:—What type of weeping is that ? What is its character ?

L:—That weeping proceeds from the heart even as a man in distress weeps sincerely from the heart for the removal of distress.

S:—I understand. I wish I could weep like this, but it does not always proceed from the heart.

L:—This shows that you seek it from the intellect, and not from the heart.

S:—O Lord, if the heart begins to seek it, why should I pray to You ? I solicit Your aid because there is no seeking from the heart.

L:—My aid can be gained when one is devoted to carrying out My instructions. Believe that the most difficult task can be easily accomplished when one is attentive to this.

S:—Lord, I shall certainly do as You ask me to do, but the progress will assuredly depend on Your grace. I am only an instrument. Therefore, knowing this to be Your instruction I shall make a special effort to carry it out. As an instrument, please make me do, whatever You desire me to do.

L:—Take care that this view may not lead you to self-deception.

S:—O Lord, can there be any deception in asking for aid from You.

L:—While seeking aid, if one avoids labour and trouble to the body, and does not carry out instructions, it means practice of deception. Fixing the mind on Me go on carrying out whatever I said. Do not contemplate on what happened in the past or will happen in future. Go on observing whatever comes to pass as a disinterested observer. This is what is called practice of surrender. Believe that everything is possible of attainment through the practice of this form of surrender.

S:—I have faith in this, but agitation caused by distress makes me forget it and the attention is automatically dragged to the goal of attainment of supreme peace and supreme bliss.

L:—Why not devote your attention exclusively to the work itself, as you devote it to the fruit of action ? When My instructions are sincerely carried out, it leads to the growth of Faith and Love and ultimately to My realization.

S:—But, O Lord, without the growth of Faith and Love in You even the carrying out of Your instructions does not become possible.

L:—You already possess the amount of Faith and Love necessary for carrying out My instructions.

S:—Then, why do I fail to carry out Your instructions to the latter ?

L:—Stored up impressions of past sins, worldly love, hatred, lust, anger and similar other evils act as obstacles.

S:—How are these to be annihilated ?

L:—I have already said that these are annihilated by practices like Bhajana, meditation, selfless service and Satsaṅga.

S:—I shall try to make special effort to devote myself to these practices. But success in this also will depend on Your grace.

L:—You may get any amount of aid you may seek from Me.

* * * *

S:—O Lord, some people say that the vision of God is gained only through the eyes of Knowledge and not through physical eyes. What is the truth about this ?

L:—What they say is not correct. In the manner a devotee wants to see Me. I can manifest Myself before him.

S:—Your form being Divine, how is it possible for the physical eyes to see the same ?

L:—Through My grace. I give him such power with the aid of which he can see My Divine form even with the physical eyes.

S:—When You manifest Your Divine form, do all the people present at the place gain Your sight, or only a select few among them?

L:—It may happen, as I desire it to happen.

S:—Physical sight is equally possessed by all, then how does it happen that some people see You, and others do not ?

L:—There is nothing to wonder in this. Through the application of Yogic power even a Yogī can act like this. Though present before a multitude, he may be actually seen by some, and not by others.

S:—When You appear before a crowd of people, do all men in the crowd see You as possessing the same form, or You appear differently before different persons.

L:—I can appear both as possessing the same form as well as in different forms before different persons. This happens according to the qualification of the observer. In other words, whatever the thoughts of the devotee, or the character of his Love and Faith, I appear so before him.

S:—How do observers remain deficient in faith even when You are directly manifested before them ? Please explain this with illustration.

L:—I can manifest Myself before a multitude though the people comprising it may be deficient in faith, or may even lack the same. And when I am manifested, people may look upon Me some with more faith and some with less. This is illustrated by My manifestation in Universal Form in the court of Duryodhana, where I was seen by people according to their thoughts and sentiments and many people could not even see Me.

S:—When You appear on earth as an incarnation, people must see You as possessing a Form which is same to all.

L:—At the time of incarnation also, I appear to people according to the nature of their thought.*

S:—Some people say that God, Who is the embodiment

---

* जाकी रही भावना जैसी। प्रभु मूरति देखी तिन तैसी॥

"Whatever was the conception of the person, the Lord's Form appeared so to him."

of Existence, Knowledge and Bliss cannot manifest Himself before a devotee assuming a definite Form. The devotees see their own thoughts reflected in the Form of their respective deities.

L:—They say so out of error. They do not know the secret of my Form with attributes. Although I am Myself embodiment of Existence, Knowledge and Bliss, through my own Yogic power I manifest Myself in My Divine Form with attributes for the sake of My devotees. Some Sādhakas may no doubt in the course of their practice imagine that they have seen Me through the projection of their mental picture, but that is not regarded as genuine Divine vision.

S:—How is a Sādhaka to understand whether his vision is genuine, or a mere projection of his mental picture ?

L:—There is a world of difference between direct Divine vision and a mental conception. When a Sādhaka directly realizes Me, he will develop all the marks of a devotee, and whatever incidents happen at the time will leave their proofs, such as when Dhruva realized Me he attained all knowledge of the scriptures as soon as his chin was touched with the conch, and when I revealed Myself for the sake of Prahlāda, I destroyed Hiraṇyakaśipu. These incidents can never be considered as mere imaginations. But when there is a realization of My form only through the imagination the incidents connected therewith will leave no proofs.

S:—Some say that God being all-pervading, how is it possible for Him to reveal Himself in a particular point of space ? Does not such manifestation refute His all-pervading character ?

L:—No, it does not. Fire is all-pervading, and yet a person desiring it lights it either at one place or in many places, as the case may be, and the god of Fire without losing his all-pervading character, manifests himself at one particular place or in many places. My pervasiveness is deeper and My power infinitely stronger than that of Fire. Where is, then, any cause for wonder if I, the all-pervading Being, while remaining present everywhere, manifest Myself with all my power intact at one place, or simultaneously in many places ?

S:—While You are absolute and Formless, how do You appear assuming a Divine Form with attributes ?

L:—Even in a clear sky water exists in the form of atoms, that water comes down as a shower and it is this very water which is, again, transformed into solid flakes and hails. Similarly, though I am above both the states of Sat and Asat, being and non-being, I am cognizable by the intellect sharpened and purified by divine knowledge. Thereafter though eternally existing as pure Knowledge and Bliss when I manifest Myself by My power of Yoga as Divine Light, I appear in the hearts of the Yogīs as a brilliant flame and then remaining as flame I manifest Myself in My Divine Form with attributes and grace my devotee with a direct vision of that Form, even as the sun when manifested spreads his light over all eyes and gives all the privilege of his sight.

S:—Some say that water being a form of matter, can undergo these transformations; but this is not possible in the case of the changeless soul or Spirit.

L:—These changes do not take place in Me, the changeless Spirit. They show only the effect of My power. I may make possible what is evidently impossible. There is absolutely nothing which is incapable of being made possible by Me.

S:—Tell me, Lord, what is the best means of obtaining Your direct vision ?

L:—Exclusive devotion to Me, or complete surrender.

S:—What are the qualifications a devotee must gain through the practice of exclusive devotion before You meet him ?

L:—When he gains the Divine qualifications *(Gītā* XVI. 1—3).

S:—Do You meet him only after he has developed all the marks defined as Divine qualifications, or even before ?

L:—There is no hard and fast rule that he must possess all the Divine qualifications before realization; but possession of exclusive devotion is indispensable.

S:—Inasmuch as You meet him only when there is exclusive devotion, and even when the divine qualifications are not fully developed, these latter must flower in him subsequent to Your realization.

L:—Not only these, but many other special virtues then flower in him.

S:—What are those special virtues ?

L:—Equanimity, etc. *(Gītā* XII. 13—20).

S:—Do these virtues appear only after Your realization, or even before ?

L:—They appear to a certain extent even before, but after My realization they flower as a matter of course.

S:—What should the devotee do for Your realization ?

L:—I have already said that he should completely surrender himself to Me.

S:—Why do You not Yourself take him under Your shelter and make him surrender himself to You ?

L:—It is not My duty to enforce surrender in a devotee. The duty of the devotee lies in surrendering himself to Me of his own accord.

S:—Do you extend any help to those who desire to surrender themselves out of reasoning and discrimination ?

L:—He who seeks help out of a sincere heart certainly receives it.

S:—Can worldly prosperity, supernatural powers, the celestials and other beings of the subtle world put any obstacle in the spiritual progress of one who desires to surrender himself to You for Your realization ?

L:—None of these can put any obstacle in his path.

S:—It is generally found that those who cultivate devotion to You have to face many dangers and difficulties in life, which sometimes act as hindrances in their spiritual path.

L:—They have not exclusively surrendered themselves to Me.

S:—Do they gain the supernatural powers after Your realization ?

L:—The devotee has no need for them.

S:—Can the devotee gain them, if he so desires ?

L:—My devotee can never cherish any desire for them and if he does he has not exclusively surrendered himself to Me.

S:—After Your realization what right or privilege is gained by Your devotee ?

L:—He does neither believe he has gained any right, nor does he seek to gain any.

S:—May You not grant him some privilege, even if he may not seek it ?

L:—Yes, I grant it to him when it is required for serving any necessity of Mine.

S:—Have You also any necessity, Lord ?

L:—Yes, I have. Propagation of the ideas of religion and devotion to God, etc., is necessary for the good of the world. That is My necessity.

S:—How much privilege do You grant him at the time ?

L:—It depends on the amount of work I have to take from him.

S:—Do You grant this privilege to all Your devotees, or to only a select few among them ?

L:—Except Sādhakas who are passive or indifferent, I may grant the privilege to all those who are prepared and willing to accept it with pleasure.

S:—Whom do You regard as qualified to receive the privilege in its entirety for the propagation of ideas of religion, right conduct and devotion ? What is the character of the devotee to whom You may grant the whole privilege ?

L:—I may grant this privilege in its entirety to the loving and supremely compassionate devotee of a generous nature whose nature is to sacrifice his all spontaneously for the good of others, whose thoughts ever flow towards others' good, and whoever feels and remains happy in the happiness of others.

S:—Do not, then, all Your devotees develop the same character and qualifications after Your realization ?

L:—No, they do not. Whatever character they show at the

time of their spiritual practice, they generally maintain even after realization. The common factor is that there is a total absence of modifications like joy and grief, attraction and repulsion, lust and anger, etc., among them. Qualifications like equanimity, peace and bliss are found equally among them, and they never do anything in contravention of the injunctions of the scriptures. Though all their activities follow the lines laid down by Me (in the scriptures), they are all the same different in every individual case.

S:—What is the reason for this difference in their external activities ?

L:—Some possess the nature of doing spiritual practice in retirement and some of doing service. These external activities differ according to the differences of nature, pre-determined Karma and intellect of the devotees, as well as differences of place, time and circumstances.

S:—In that case, he is the best among them to whom You may grant the full privilege.

L:—Use of comparison is out of place here. All of them are best. He who is by nature inclined towards activities is specially entrusted with the responsibility to work.

S:—All should feel an equal enthusiasm in carrying out a work enjoined by You.

L:—It is true that all of them feel an equal enthusiasm in carrying out my work, but I distribute the work according to their nature. There are some who love to remain constantly by My side, I, therefore, do not send them out. I entrust him with service of the people who is inclined to that form of service. One who is inclined to the life of a recluse, I generally do not entrust with any work. I distribute the work according to the nature and capacity of the devotee.

S:—The devotee should develop the nature that You may entrust any special work to him without any hesitation. What are the best means of developing this nature ?

L:—Complete and wholehearted surrender to Me alone.

S:—Kindly explain for our benefit what is meant by complete surrender ?

L:—Constant remembrance of, and meditation on, My Name and Form with consciousness of their virtues and power, carrying out of My instructions for My pleasure without break in remembrance and remaining ever happy in My dispensation.

S:—O Lord, meditation on Your Form appeals to my heart also. But the mind is unsteady. It runs away quickly hither and thither. How shall I account for this ?

L:—Owing to attachment the mind finds a pleasure in the enjoyment of worldly things. It has become a store of the impressions of Karma of many lives. These do not allow the mind to become steady.

S:—Why does it dwell on useless things which serve no purpose of mine and for which I have no particular attachment ?

L:—By nature the mind is fickle and unsteady. It is its habit to dwell on useless things and it finds a pleasure in such thoughts. This is also a form of attachment, that is why it dwells on such thoughts.

S:—What is to be done to remedy this ?

L:—The mind should be carefully watched that it may not leave the meditation of My Form and take to thoughts of worldly things. If that is not sufficient to prevent the continuation of such thoughts, it should be expostulated or forcibly withdrawn from such thoughts, and employed again and again with determination in the meditation of My Form.

S:—How can the mind be withdrawn from thoughts of other things ?

L:—When a small child picks up a sharp knife, the mother expostulates with the child and removes the knife from its hands. If the child due to ignorance and foolishness begins to resist the mother, the mother will be indifferent to its cries and forcibly take away the knife. Even so, the mind should be remonstrated and cured of its habit of pursuing worldly thoughts; for it is as fickle and unsteady as a small child. It does not and cannot consider the harm its vagaries may bring one in the future.

S:—One may not even know when the mind will give him the slip and quickly grasp an object. What should one do to remedy this ?

L:—Just as a mother constantly keeps watch over her child, even so the mind should be watched.

S:—But the mind is fickle, strong and wayward, therefore it appears extremely difficult to control it.

L:—True, it is somewhat difficult to control, but not so difficult as you imagine it to be. For it can be brought under control through effort. The difficulty of the task should not make one despair. The mother never considers the task of protecting her child difficult. If she does so, the protection of her child will be impossible.

S:—Is the mind exactly like a small child ?

L:—No, it is stronger and more wayward than a child.

S:—Then, how is it to be brought under control ?

L:—It can be brought under control, for the intellect is more powerful than the mind and you (the soul) is still more powerful. Just as a mother controls her small child either with the help of a grown-up daughter or holding some temptation before it, and if the child still persists to be wayward she changes its course from evil to good by a show of threat, even so, the mind has to be restrained through the intellect by showing it the evil effects of a life of enjoyment. Thus withdrawing it from the perishable, transient objects of the world, it should be fixed again and again on Me.

S:—However much I may try on this line, I do not see any prospect of victory.

L:—Persevere, even if you do not attain victory. Do not get depressed. When you have My support, there is no cause for despair. Have faith that if you continue the fight, ultimately the victory is sure to be yours.

S:—O Lord, when I retire to a solitary place and attempt to fix the mind in meditation on You, sleep and lethargy begin to trouble me. Please tell me what I should do to get over this difficulty ?

L:—The food you take should be light and pure. You should sit still in a Yogic posture, e.g., the Lotus or Svastika posture without feeling any inconvenience, keeping your spine erect and fixing the sight on the tip of the nose. Then you should offer prayers and chant hymns in praise of Me. You should go on repeatedly chanting and bringing to your mind whatever you have heard from the lips of the saints and read in the scriptures about the glory of My Name, Form, virtues, sports and powers. This will cause the growth of the pure Sattvic sentiment and bring awakening to the intellect. When this awakening takes place, sleep and lethargy, which are the expressions of Tamoguṇa, cannot exercise any influence.

S:—O Lord, you have said in the *Gītā* that Your realization becomes easy when one takes to constant remembrance of You, for You then quickly deliver one from the ocean of metempsychosis by giving protection to his spiritual practices and remedying the deficiencies in them. But it does not appear to me that Your realization is so easy or can be achieved so quickly as You describe it to be.

L:—You do not practise constant remembrance of Me, therefore My realization appears difficult to you.

S:—I admit, Lord, that what You say is true. Through constant remembrance of You, Your realization may be both quick and easy. But constant remembrance itself is a difficult affair. How is this habit to be developed ?

L:—The practice of constant remembrance appears difficult to you because you do not know My virtues, power, truth and mystery. As a matter of fact, it is not so difficult.

S:—Please tell me what are Your virtues, power, truth and mystery.

L:—Equanimity, peace, compassion, love, forbearance,

sweetness, tenderness, gravity, liberality, friendliness, etc., these are My virtues. Entire greatness, strength, glory, brilliance, power, ability and the capacity to render possible what is otherwise impossible—these are My glory. Just as atoms of water, steam, cloud, drops of rain, hail, etc., all are but different forms of water, even so whatever exists, with attributes and without attributes, with form and without form, manifest and unmanifest, matter and spirit, animate and inanimate, and whatever is beyond these, all are but Me. This is the truth about Me. To believe that through My very sight, through the hearing of My voice, through My touch, remembrance, Kīrtana, worship, obeisance and offering of praises to Me, even a sinner gets exceptionally pure; and to recognize Me, the Supreme, Omniscient, Almighty Being, though equally present everywhere, yet walking as a human being in the form of an Incarnation—this is My mystery or secret.

S:—How are these to be known ?

L:—In the beginning of its career in school, a small child tries to avoid learning its lessons, but with the growth of age and experience when it comes to realize the virtue, glory, truth and secret of learning, it begins to engage itself in study with great devotion and enthusiasm. Then, it would not leave its study even when asked to do so. Similarly through Satsaṅga or association with the good, and practices of Bhajana, meditation, etc., man can learn My virtues, glory, secret, etc. Then he attains such an amount of joy and peace that he would not leave it even if requested to do so.

S:—O Lord, when engaged in Your constant remembrance, is it possible for a man to engage his body and senses to work according to Your instructions ?

L:—Through determined practice it is possible. Though the mind of the tortoise is concentrated on its eggs, of the cow on its calf, of a lustful person on his lady love, of a greedy man on his wealth, of the chauffeur driving a car on the road before him, of a rope-dancer on the balance of his feet, yet they carry on other activities through their bodies and senses, even so, it is possible for a Sādhaka to carry on external activities through the body and senses, according to My instructions, while engaged in constant remembrance of Me.

S:—What are Your instructions ?

L:—Elevating scriptures, sayings of saints, good impulses bubbling up within the heart—these are My instructions. When differences are observed in these three, one should adopt a course in which two of them agree, regarding that to be My instruction.

S:—What should be done when the opinions of all the three are found to be different ?

L:—In that case, the saying of a saint should be given preference.

S:—Would it not mean disrespect to the scriptures ?

L:—No, the saint can never say anything which is contrary to the scriptures. It is difficult for the ordinary man to determine the meaning of the scriptures; the saint alone knows the application of a scriptural instruction according to time and place. That is why whatever is shown by the saint is the right path.

S:—What is the harm if one regards the good impulses of the heart as a Divine injunction ?

L:—One may do so. But the impulses should correspond to the instructions of the scriptures and sayings of saints. It is necessary for a Sādhaka to submit himself to a discipline, for otherwise if due to ignorance he begins to regard the Rajasic and Tamasic impulses as Sattvic in character, he may lose all restraint and suffer a spiritual fall.

S:—What do You mean by scriptures here ?

L:—All books composed by the Ṛsis, *e.g.,* the Śrutis, Smṛtis, Itihāsas and Purāṇas, etc., are scriptures. In case of difference of view between two books of scripture, preference should be given to the Śrutis. For the Smṛtis, Itihāsas and Purāṇas—all these are based on the Śrutis.

S:—It is difficult for ordinary men to acquire knowledge of the Śrutis, Smṛtis and all other scriptures. By what should they go under the circumstance ?

L:—They should depend on Mahāpuruṣas who have knowledge of the scriptures.

S:—Who should be regarded as a Mahāpuruṣa ?

L:—He whom you regard from your heart as the best of men is a Mahāpuruṣa for you.

S:—O Lord, I may make a mistake in my judgment and may be deceived thereby.

L:—You need not worry over this. He who surrenders himself to Me, receives My protection from all points of view.

S:—O Lord, what is the standard by which I shall judge a Mahāpuruṣa ? What are the marks of a Mahāpuruṣa ?

L:—The great soul in which the marks described in the *Gītā* chapter II, verses 55—71 as the marks of a man of stable wisdom, chapter VI, verses 7—9 as marks of a Yogī, chapter XII, verses 13—19 as marks of a devotee, chapter XIV, verses 22—25 as marks of one who has risen above the guṇas are found is a Mahāpuruṣa.

S:—It is most difficult to come in contact with such a Mahāpuruṣa. What is to be done under the circumstance ?

L:—In that case the *Gītā* which contains My instructions to Arjuna and is the essence of all scriptures and easy to understand by all, should be made the guide.

S:—What are the verses which should be principally kept in view by the Sādhaka while developing his virtues and regulating his conduct ?

L:—There are many verses in the *Gītā* which can be made one's guide. One's life should be regulated particularly according to verses 7 to 11 of chapter XIII where wisdom is described, verses 1 to 3 of chapter XVI where the divine qualities are described, and verses 14 to 17 of chapter XVII where penances are described.

S:—O Lord, You have said that one should ever remain pleased with every dispensation of Yours. What do You really mean by this ?

L:—It means one should feel delighted through every experience of life, viz., pleasure or pain, gain or loss, experience agreeable or disagreeable, taking it to be a gift specially sent by Me.

S:—Pleasure is not always felt when these experiences are gone through. What is the reason for this ?

L:—People do not know this truth and secret that every dispensation of Mine is an expression of My compassion.

S:—Pleasurable possessions of the world like wife, children, wealth, a comfortable house, etc., create infatuation and attachment and cause bondage to man. Why do You make man possessor of these things ? In what way is the secret of Your compassion to be detected in this dispensation ?

L:—Just as a king when calling a friend sends a car to bring him, even so as the result of past virtues I make man possessor of worldly objects like wife, children, wealth, house, etc., for service of others and making others happy and for the growth of right conduct, virtues and Love for Me so that he may sooner come to Me. To understand this is to know the secret of My grace.

S:—When wife, children, wealth, etc., are lost, how is Your grace to be detected in their loss ?

L:—When due to infatuation and attachment insects fall into a flame and are reduced to ashes, a kind-hearted man observing their miserable plight puts out the flame. Although the insects may not know it, the action is an expression of supreme compassion for them. Even so, it should be known to be an act of My supreme grace when objects of enjoyment, which cause bondage to man and drag him down to hell, are destroyed.

S:—Why do You endow man with health, strength and

intellectual power, etc. ?

L:—I endow man with these powers so that he may know My virtues, glory, truth and secret through Satsaṅga, selfless service and constant practice of Bhajana and meditation etc.

S:—How is one to see Your grace when afflicted with illness, danger etc. ?

L:—Through the experience of illness, danger etc., man works out the effects of previous sin, and sorrow or the bitter experience of life acts as a check to the commission of sin in future. Fear of death causes dispassion for the body and aids My remembrance. If the sufferings of a disease are gone through in the spirit of performing a penance, they may lead to My realization. The development of this attitude means seeing My grace.

S:—Your grace is apparent when one contacts a Mahāpuruṣa, but how is Your grace to be seen when one loses that contact.

L:—Man realizes the value of a light when the light is removed from him. When contact with a Mahāpuruṣa is lost, it should be understood that I arrange this in order to develop in him desire to meet him again, and develop love for him and I make the Sādhaka realize how rare and treasurable is the contact with a Mahāpuruṣa.

S:—Your grace is apparent when You bring about separation from wicked men of evil conduct for thereby You save one from evil association. But why do You throw one into evil company even against one's desire or inclination ?

L:—I throw one into such association in order to give him an idea of the evil effects of vice, so that he may develop distaste for vice and evil conduct. But remember, when one deliberately cultivates evil association, it is not arranged by Me.

S:—How is Your grace to be seen during association with, and separation from ordinary men ?

L:—Association with them is arranged for their service and for cultivation of love and compassion for them and separation is arranged for cultivation of detachment for them and for constant practice of Bhajana and meditation in seclusion. To understand this is to see My grace.

S:—How is Your grace to be seen in difficulties like entanglement in civil or criminal suits, which disturb moral principles and practices of Bhajana and meditation.

L:—The practices of morality, Bhajana and meditation are disturbed when one is subject to lust, anger, greed, infatuation, fear, weakness etc. He who looks upon these difficulties as gifts from Me, and while facing them does not fall from morality and rectitude, virtues like firmness, courage, gravity etc., which lead to the growth of soulforce, increase in him. To understand this is to see My grace.

S:—Why do You deprive a devotee of worldly honour, name and fame ? What is the secret of it ?

L:—I do so with a view to awaken him from the sleep of Ignorance, to remove the hindrances in the path of his spiritual Sādhanā, and displacing hypocrisy, to develop in him devotion in its genuine form. This is the secret.

S:—What is the special form of Your grace ?

L:—Memory of, and desire for, and actual practice of Bhajana, meditation, selfless service, Satsaṅga, virtues and right conduct—these are the special forms of My grace.

S:—When such is the case, one should treat all these dispensations of Yours, arranged according to one's Karma, as gifts from You, and feel charmed and delighted every moment.

L:—That is so, but the pity is that people do not understand it.

S:—What should one do to understand this ?

L:—One should constantly remember My Name and Form with consciousness of their power and glory, practice disinterested Karma according to My instructions maintaining My remembrance and associate with saints who have knowledge of the secret of My grace.

Desirability of Faith in Dharma and God

Dharma is that which ensures sublime joy, peace and thriving success here as well as hereafter and finally leads to the attainment of matchless, supreme, beatific, eternal and unalloyed happiness.* And God is that eternally existent conscious principle which brings forth, sustains and dissolves the universe and the various orders of living beings inhabiting it, controls their destinies, provides for their joys and sorrows and regulates the world-process according to the Karmas of the different Jīvas. 'Śāstra' or scripture is the collective name of the body of injunctions and prohibitions promulgated, in accordance with the spirit of the Vedas, (which possess a divine authority) by the all-knowing Ṛṣis or seers, who are believed to know the will and intention of God. Endowed with faith in God he who conducts himself in accordance with the scriptural injunctions attains in the end the supreme and final goal of human existence in the form of God-Realization, enjoying sublime peace, happiness and prosperity in this world as well. This is the supreme gain that follows from the observance of Dharma.

The all-round and steady progress of the world depend on Dharma and God alone. Dharma always rests on God; and where Dharma abides, God is undoubtedly there. The two are inseparably bound up with each other. Dharma is nothing but the law of God. And victory ever attends upon Dharma.

यतः कृष्णस्ततो धर्मो यतो धर्मस्ततो जयः ।

When man ceases to have faith in God and Dharma, the bond of Dharma gets relaxed and he begins to conduct himself according to his own sweet will. And he who acts as he pleases

---

* यतोऽभ्युदयनिःश्रेयससिद्धिः स धर्मः । *(Vaiśeṣika-Sūtras)*

य एव श्रेयस्करः स एव धर्मशब्देनोच्यते। *(Gloss on the Mīmāṁsā-Sūtras)*

attains neither success nor the highest goal, nor even happiness. The Lord says in the *Gītā:—*

यः शास्त्रविधिमुत्सृज्य वर्तते कामकारतः ।
न स सिद्धिमवाप्नोति न सुखं न परां गतिम् ॥

(XVI.23)

Success in this world and happiness as also the supreme state can be attained only through the observance of Dharma. The fact that failure and misery are met with everywhere in the world today clearly indicates that man has fallen from virtue—he has lost faith in God and does not act according to His injunctions. The suffering of the world will not come to an end so long as man refuses to believe in God and His laws and continues to act according to his own will. We all seek success in our undertakings, but it is idle to expect success with one's back turned on God and Dharma.

We are told in the *Gītā* how at the beginning of creation Brahmā, the Creator of the world, enjoined man that he should propitiate the gods through sacrifice in the shape of performing his own duty (Svadharma) and that pleased with and fostered by his services the gods should in their turn foster him and help his advancement—'देवान् भावयतानेन ते देवा भावयन्तु वः'. If the gods cease to help and nourish us, our life will become impossible in this world, and in order to receive help from them it is obligatory on us to foster them in return. The grim holocaust that we witness all-round in the world today through wars, epidemics, excessive rains, droughts, famines, earthquakes, fires and floods etc., is solely attributable to the fact that man has ceased to foster the gods. Even today the gods are not so negligent towards us as we have grown delinquent towards them. The sun rises and sets at regular intervals even today. The moon still sheds nectar on us and our crops and plants as heretofore. Fire gives us heat and light as ever before and serves us in so many ways. Their functions are undoubtedly showing some signs of irregularity, but their nature has not yet changed. It is said of them that as soon as their nature changes the dissolution of the world will follow. Therefore, in order to advance to prosperity and happiness of the world it is quite imperative that the gods should be worshipped and fostered. In the secular sphere success is speedily attained by offering worship and sacrifices to the gods. The Lord says in the *Gītā:—*

काङ्क्षन्तः कर्मणां सिद्धिं यजन्त इह देवताः ।
क्षिप्रं हि मानुषे लोके सिद्धिर्भवति कर्मजा ॥

(IV.12)

"In this world of human beings, men seeking fruition of their activities worship the gods; for success born of actions follows quickly."

Here it is noteworthy that while on the one hand the Lord declares that one cannot attain success through actions performed according to one's own sweet will, He promises on the other hand quick success to those who worship the gods. This proves the desirability and efficacy of offering worship to the gods even for success in worldly affairs.

Performance of the five daily sacrifices—Pañcamahāyajñas is an important part of the rites prescribed for propitiating the gods. This consists of offering worship to the gods. Ṛṣis, Manes, human beings and other living beings; the rite known as 'Balivaiśvadeva' (in which morsels of cooked food are offered to all the principal deities through the fire before meals) stands as a symbol for all the five sacrifices. In these sacrifices the gods are propitiated through oblations to the sacred fire and worship, the Ṛṣis through the study of the Vedas, the Manes through the offering of water, men through hospitality, and other beings by offering morsels of food etc. To say nothing of performing the Pañcamahāyajñas, people do not even regularly observe the daily obligation of performing Sandhyā (the morning and evening prayers). On the other hand, they indulge in practices which instead of nourishing and fostering the gods tend to weaken their power. That mankind should occasionally fall a prey to natural calamities under such circumstances, is not to be wondered at. The man of today has lost faith in religious practices; it is therefore that he thinks of no other course beyond trying the secular means. The so-called educated men of today take exception to the performance of sacrifices arguing that at the present moment when the country is faced with a serious food crisis and people are dying of starvation for want of food, wasting such large quantities of foodgrains by consigning them to the fire in the name of religion is nothing short of an egregious crime. But they do not pause to consider where these foodgrains come from. The whole stock of our provisions we get from Mother Earth. Again, for the production of foodgrains showers are indispensible. But we cannot get showers but for the grace of Indra, the rain-god. Under such circumstances, just as the sowing of seeds for getting a good return is not misusing them, even so offering oblations of food and ghee to the sacred fire with a view to fostering the gods can never be called a waste. It is rather supremely essential for the welfare of humanity. If the gods are duly worshipped natural calamities like famines and epidemics can never visit us. And Mother Earth will yield us an inexhaustible store of food materials.

The immortal Tulasīdāsa has sung of the happy state of the land during the ideal reign of Bhagavān Śrī Rāma in the following strain:—

"The trees and creepers yielded honey for the mere asking; And the cows, young and docile, discharged delicious milk in abundance. The land was ever rich with bumper crops, in Tretā appeared Satyayuga with all its glory.

The teeming mountains brought forth treasures of precious stones and jewels, Knowing the Ruler of the Earth to be none else than the Universal Spirit. Cool, limpid and fragrant water playfully flowed in the rivers bounteous. And the fathomless oceans never did venture to transgress their bounds.

They served the people with pearls and gems poured forth in profusion on their banks.

The beautiful lakes and ponds did abound in lotuses of various kinds.

In sooth the quarters all-round presented a glorious and jubilant sight.

The moon bathed the land in her silvery nectarous rays.

The sun shone bright, gave heat and light in response to time.

The impregnate clouds showered when in demand in the kingdom of Lord Śrī Rāma."

The poet attributes all this to the observance of Dharma. He says:—

"Treading the path of the Vedas, each one was devoted to duty as prescribed for one's order in society and stage in life.

So all enjoyed the felicity of life:

Fear, sorrow or disease were unknown there."

The moderns may dismiss this picture as a mere myth or hyperbole; but really such is not the case. The goodwill of those forces which run the wheel of creation can bring even the impossible into the region of possibility. In this case, however, Bhagavān Śrī Rāma, the crestjewel among the Raghus, was God Himself. He was the repository of infinite powers. If such was the state of affairs under His divine regime there is nothing to be wondered at. Such is the belief, nay, experience of religious-minded men. In their opinion secular means are not so effective as religious practices. The only way to see a tree rich with foliage is to water it at its root. By watering a tree at its roots we not only nourish its trunk, boughs and branches, but its very twigs, stems, leaves and fruits as well. If instead of watering a tree at its root we water its branches, stems, leaves and fruits alone it will be of no avail and the tree instead of putting on green foliage will soon get dry and perish. To resort to external means alone rather than perform the obligatory duty of worshipping God and propitiating the other deities in obedience to His commandments for advancing peace and prosperity in the world and averting natural calamities is as good as watering the leaves of a tree rather than its roots.

The exertion of man in the external material field is not inconsiderable today. One cannot say if the amenities of life and physical comforts that are available today existed ever before. Being impediments in the way of spiritual progress, material enjoyments were not made much of in those days. But the conduct of the present-day man is just like watering the branches and leaves of a tree rather than its roots. That is why his efforts instead of being crowned with success prove futile. The more we resort to external means for attaining peace and happiness, the more is the world drifting towards misery and unrest.

It is wrong to say that people have no time to offer worship to the gods. Time they have got; but a large majority of the people have lost faith in practices intended to propitiate superhuman agencies. Where there is faith, time can easily be found. People are never short of time for visiting cinemas, addressing public meetings and attending social functions and indulging in various sorts of undesirable recreations and relaxations in clubs and joining dinners. Such was not the case in olden days. Even the biggest of emperors devoted a part of their time to the worship of gods and other religious duties. The daily performance of Sandhyā (morning and evening prayers), Tarpaṇa (offering of water to the gods, Ṛṣis and manes), Balivaiśvadeva (offering a portion of the daily meal to all creatures and another to the gods through the fire, before partaking of it). Gāyatrī-Japa (repeating the sacred formula known as Gāyatrī) and Agnihotra (offering oblations to the sacred fire) etc., was looked upon as obligatory for members of the twice-born classes (men invested with the sacred thread). We read in the *Mahābhārata* that while proceeding to the forest having lost his all in a game of dice Yudhiṣṭhira was accompanied by the sacrificial fires. Nay, even in the thick of a battle when the shades of dusk fell on the two contending armies and in the event of the issue of the battle remaining inconclusive fighting was stopped for the day by mutual agreement, and the belligerents on both sides sat down to say their evening prayers. The story of King Dilīpa tells us how that famous emperor laid aside his kingly dignity and roamed about in the forest tending the heifer of his preceptor like an ordinary servant under the latter's orders. We find an account of Śrī Kṛṣṇa's daily routine in the *Bhāgavata*. It is mentioned there that He woke up in the concluding watch of the night, washing His hands and feet and rinsing His mouth He would sit down for meditation on the Self. After that He would take a plunge bath in a tank with due ceremony, have a pair of clothes, perform Sandhyā (morning prayers) and Agnihotra (offering oblations into the sacred fire) and then silently repeat the sacred Gāyatrī Mantra. He would then stand before the rising Sun to utter prayers to the sun-god and would offer oblations of water to the gods, Ṛṣis and Manes who are but part manifestations of Himself. Thereafter He would offer worship to the Brāhmaṇas and bestow on them gifts of wearing apparel and sesamum seeds alongwith 13,084 cows duly caparisoned and decked with ornaments everyday. Then He would offer obeisance to cows, the Brāhmaṇas, gods and other superiors as well as to the elders of the family (vide Book X. chapter 70 of the *Bhāgavata*). In this way a considerable part of Śrī Kṛṣṇa's time, everyday, was spent in the performance of religious duties. Whose life can be so full of activity as that of Śrī Kṛṣṇa ? Yet He spent six hours regularly every morning in the performance of religious duties. But why did He do all this ? The answer to this questions is furnished by Himself. In the *Gītā* He says:—

"Arjuna, there is nothing in all the three worlds for Me to do, nor is there anything worth attaining unattained by Me; yet I continue to work. Should I not engage in action, scrupulously at any time, great harm will come to the world; for Arjuna, men follow My way in all matters. If I cease to act, these worlds will perish; nay, I should prove to be the cause of confusion, and of the destruction of these people."*

Really speaking people in those days relied more on divine help than on worldly means. While the former of the two can be compared to watering the roots of a tree, the latter is analogous to watering its leaves. To say nothing of the religious-minded public, even great desperadoes like Hiraṇyākṣa, Hiraṇyakaśipu, Rāvaṇa and Kumbhakarṇa, believed in austerities and sacrifices, no matter however wicked their motive might have been. Hiraṇyakaśipu propitiated Brahmā by his unparalleled austerities; while Rāvaṇa offered his heads in sacrifice to Bhagavān Śiva severing them with his own hands and secured an unfailing boon from Him. It is equally true that they abused the power attained through the propitiation of the gods and incurred the displeasure of the Lord through their unpious acts and eventually lost their irresistible power and all that they possessed, nay, their beloved life as well. But as their beginning was noble they were privileged to meet their end at the hands of the Lord and finally attained supreme blessedness. Their life too teaches us the lesson that even as we acquire power through austerity and worship of the gods we lose the same through unrighteous conduct.

Power can be acquired through worldly means as well; but

* न मे पार्थास्ति कर्तव्यं त्रिषु लोकेषु किंचन।
नानवाप्तमवाप्तव्यं वर्त एव च कर्मणि॥
यदि ह्यहं न वर्तेयं जातु कर्मण्यतन्द्रितः।
मम वर्त्मानुवर्तन्ते मनुष्याः पार्थ सर्वशः॥

(*Gītā* III. 22-23)

such power does not endure. To what heights of power did Germany rise in a comparatively short time; but today the whole country has gone to rack and ruin. Europe is considered to be, nay it actually stands, at the zenith of prosperity today; but the unrest and turmoil that prevail there are known only to the people inhabiting that continent. America is recognized as the most powerful and prosperous nation of the present-day world but there is no peace or happiness even there. Fed up with their agitated life many people are heard committing suicide. Feelings of Love and hatred and the spirit of revenge are also rampant among them. Nay, in numerous cases even husbands and wives enter into litigation with each other. Japan rose into eminence so soon that it began to be counted among the biggest powers of the world. But the sad plight to which it has been reduced today is known to all. The failure that is eventually met with in this way is due to the unrighteousness of one's endeavours. An unrighteous act may appear to be attended with success in the beginning but it invariably meets with failure in the end. An unrighteous endeavour not only proves futile but leads to a miserable life hereafter. Bhagavān Śrī Kṛṣṇa has in course of Chapter XVI of the *Gītā* given a very beautiful and vivid account of the demoniacal properties and the evil consequences attending them. It goes without saying that the man of today is unmistakably turning into a veritable demon; and his activities are generally of the type described by the Lord as characterizing those who possess demoniacal properties. Whether one may believe in or not, the inevitable result of all this is suffering and unrest in this world and the horrible tortures of hell in the next.

It has been pointed out above that happiness, success and supreme blessedness solely depend upon Dharma and God. But it is these two that the arrogant devilish man of today has begun to look down upon as superfluous and worth rejecting. Only a few years back the Russians had the perversity to banish even God and religion by an overwhelming majority. (Thank the Lord, the horrors of the last world war have opened their eyes and now it is gratifying to note that they no longer openly defy God or religion and religious services have been started once more in the churches there). After the fashion of the westerners we Indians too have begun to say that it is religion which has brought about our downfall, that it is faith in God which has reduced us to our present degraded position. The fact that we are no longer afraid of sin is attributable to this very belief. A believer in God and religion will hesitate to commit sin even in seclusion; for he knows that God is omnipresent and has eyes all-around. An unbeliever, on the other hand, would not shrink from sin; he would only try to elude the clutches of law. That is the reason why people commit sins of various kinds contriving ever new methods to evade the law. It is due to disbelief in Dharma and God, that bribery and corruption have grown rampant in all spheres. The execrable tendencies of blackmarketing and profiteering are also attributable to that. The Government are going to open new departments to put a stop to bribery and blackmarketing; but the officials that will be appointed to check the evil will be human beings like ourselves. Who can say that in their attempt to eradicate bribery and blackmarketing they will not fall a victim to these evils themselves and be led astray tomorrow. The position today is that even the so-called guardians of the people have begun to exploit them unreservedly. All this is due to the fact that there is no moral or religious scruple left in our minds, but nobody cares to bestow any thought on this aspect of the question. The result is that one does not hesitate to commit the worst sin in order to gain a trivial end. One may do whatever one likes provided one can avoid detection. That is why the ability to commit sin and at the same time to evade the law is taken to be a sign of wisdom. The belief that the omnipresent Divinity sees everything, and even knows what exists in our mind has almost disappeared from our minds.

There goes a story that two aspirants once approached a saint in quest of wisdom. The teacher handed over a bird to each of the two disciples and asked them to dispose of it unnoticed. One of the disciples promptly took the bird to some solitary retreat and made short work of it in obedience to the commands of the preceptor. The other one also tried his best to find out a place where he could carry out the behest of the Guru quite unnoticed; but he failed to find such a place. Wherever he went there was some one already to witness his performance. Here there was a beast and there he found a bird. Where there was no living creature, he discovered that at least the wind-god was present there. Even in a lonely wilderness it struck him that the sylvan deity must be there. Whithersoever he went, Mother Earth would be invariably present there, and so also the sun-god. Even where none else was to be seen, his own self as well as the Witness residing within his heart were unquestionably there. At last he came away disappointed; and whereas the other disciple was glorying over his achievement, he for his part lamented over his failure to carry out the behest of his preceptor and despondency was writ large on his countenance. The preceptor was not slow to find out that the latter disciple alone was truly eligible for the boon of wisdom inasmuch as he beheld the Lord everywhere. The teacher possessed superhuman powers; he restored to life the bird disposed of by the former disciple.

The long and short of it is that like the former disciple the man of today believes only in the testimony of his senses. The evil resulting from unrighteousness is not open to perception. That is why people feel no demur in telling lies, giving false evidence and making false entries in account-books etc. Even when detected they repent over their inefficiency in forgery and make up their mind to be more cautious in future. They never feel even then that they have committed sin in telling a lie, the result of which would never be favourable to them. We have fallen so low today that the educated society of the present-day has begun to look down upon all believers in God and Religion as hypocrites and fools. Nay, people have begun to hesitate in calling themselves theists in civilized society. True, there are many hypocrites too among those who call themselves theists and religious men and they are even more dangerous and greater propagators of godlessness than the so-called unbelievers. But God and Religion cannot be repudiated because of such people. Truth will ever remain truth. It cannot be set aside at any time. Of course, he who refuses to believe in it will be deprived of its benefit and will perish.

Even of such noble and tender-hearted souls as seek to alleviate the suffering of the people to diffuse peace and happiness all-round, to stamp out immorality and wrong-doing and to ensure an equal distribution of worldly objects and amenities among all, the large majority consists of those who adopt only worldly means for the realization of this end and exhort others as well to do the same. They neither undertake practices which tend to promote faith in God and Religion, the only source of peace and happiness, nor do they exhort others to undertake such practices. That is why there is such an unrest and turmoil in the whole world and the human race is being consumed by the fire of suffering.

Dhaŕma and God are eternal, constant and great. For our own well-being we should take refuge in them and make efforts to popularize them. "Dharma protects us if we stand by it," (धर्मो रक्षति रक्षितः) so says the scripture. It is the duty of the wise and the thoughtful to propagate religious ideas through pious conduct. Nobody can propagate Dharma without practising it himself. Truly speaking, no one can popularize Dharma or God. God is omnipotent. It is through His energy that everything is happening. All those who seek blessedness shall have to acknowledge Him sooner or later. There is no redemption for the soul without acknowledging Him. Nevertheless it behoves every pious and believing soul to popularize God and Dharma by his conduct. Let him advance towards Dharma and God himself and also strive to help others do the same. Herein lies the greatest service of the world and its true welfare.

Beloved of the Lord

"You may go on repeating the *Gītā* all day long and continue your efforts to mould your life according to the same; but bread also must claim a part of your attention," said the younger brother to his elder brother. The latter was ever busy reciting the *Gītā*. He had heard that the daily recitation of even a single chapter of that book with an eye to its meaning and spirit was better than reciting the whole scripture everyday. But the best thing was to mould one's life according to the *Gītā*. Besides, there are many verses in the *Gītā,* anyone of which was enough to redeem a soul if one translated it into one's daily life. The eldest of the four brothers was a lover of the *Gītā*. He was trying to follow verse 17 of Chapter XII in his actual life. He kept quiet even on hearing the above admonition of his younger brother.

"You too must exert yourself to earn money like us." observed a still younger brother.

"How long shall we feed you by our own earnings ?" put in the youngest in the same strain.

"The best solution for you is to disunite from us," blurted out the first younger brother in the heat of the moment.

"Really we shall not be able to pull together with you," added the next one in a still harsher tone.

The eldest brother calmly replied:—

"He who neither rejoices nor hates, nor grieves nor desires, and who renounces both good and evil actions and is full of devotion, is dear to Me, so says the Lord to Arjuna in the Gītā."*

---

* यो न हृष्यति न द्वेष्टि न शोचति न काङ्क्षति।
शुभाशुभपरित्यागी भक्तिमान्यः स मे प्रियः॥

"Keep this sermon to yourself. You had better secede from us this very day," the youngest brother sternly interposed.

"I neither rejoice nor grieve over the fact that you are disowning me," the *Gītā*-lover coolly replied. "I bear no grudge to you nor have I any inclination to part company with you. He alone is dear to God, who is above joy, grief, desire and ill-will. Do as you deem fit."

"He won't come to his senses until he is separated. He seeks to lead an easy life by indulging in rhetoric," the first younger brother pronounced his verdict.

"We supported him for a long time. We are now sick of him." The next one endorsed the opinion of his two rebellious brothers.

"If we continued to live together, I should have to cook food for the other three brothers too", loudly remarked the cross-tempered wife of the *Gītā*-lover from inside the house. "Let all the three secede, there is no cause for worry."

"He alone is dear to God, who does not rejoice in favourable circumstances," the *Gītā*-lover gently admonished his wife.

"You should not talk in that strain. Besides, there is no occasion for rejoicing either; for God had given you an opportunity to serve so many fellow-beings. This was a matter for congratulation to you; you ought to have been grateful to the Lord for the same."

"So many jewels, articles of wearing apparel, utensils and cash fall to your lot and the smaller house has been allotted for your residence." The three younger brothers placed a few articles before their eldest brother. They were all excited. The pungent words of their sister-in-law had inflamed their anger.

"If such is the will of God, let us bow to it," the *Gītā*-lover calmly replied. His countenance bore the same naturally cheerful and tranquil aspect. There was no trace of worry in his looks.

× × × ×

"You are still sitting idle, that won't do," the wife of the *Gītā*-lover tauntingly said. "न काङ्क्षति—the devotee craves not," was the answer. "I have no craving for money. He alone is dear to the Lord, who has no craving."

"When the cash balance is spent, how shall we be able to manage things ?" The question once more came.

"न शोचति—he does not worry," was the cut and dried reply. "The man who has no worries is a favourite with God. Hence I do not worry about my bread." The wife of the *Gītā*-lover kept mum.

× × × ×

"I have no money left with me now, what shall I do ?" The worried wife asked her husband one day.

"न काङ्क्षति—he craves not," was the same old reply.

"Not a single jewels is left on my person," the afflicted wife approached her husband once again after an interval of some days. "The whole lot has been deposited into the belly. Pray do something now."

"न शोचति—he worries not," was the set form of reply.

Having lost all hope, the wife suppressed her feelings and kept quiet.

× × × ×

"I have nothing left with me now," the wife of the *Gītā*-lover resumed her tale of woe in a mournful voice. "Our dwelling has already been sold. We are living in a hired house. I have cooked food in utensils borrowed from others. Beyond a pair of clothes on our person we have nothing left with us in the form of cash, ornaments, wearing apparel, utensils or sundries, whereon we could live. Pray do some work now at least." The wife hopefully pressed her husband.

"न काङ्क्षति—he craves not," was the usual reply.

"How shall we be able to manage things after all ?" observed the impatient lady, wiping her tears.

"न शोचति—he cares not; only such a soul is dear to God," replied the *Gītā*-lover and kept quiet.

"What a queer brain you possess," the wife peevishly observed. "I was hoping that when everything was spent up, you would surely do something. But I have got sick of hearing the same hackneyed remark. A devotee neither craves nor worries; it is such attitude that pleases the Lord."

"I am telling you the bare truth, O good lady !" the *Gītā*-lover said. This very morning when I repaired to the river-bank having answered the calls of nature, I found that the river-bed was dry on the surface and that water was still flowing below the surface. As I dug underground at the very bank for obtaining water, I discovered a bucket full of jewels and rubies and gold coins. I forthwith remembered the words of the Lord: "He who rejoices not on meeting with what is agreeable is dear to me." Hence I did not feel the least delighted on the discovery of that heap of jewels. As the Lord further says that the devotee hates not, I did not feel repelled by it either, nor did I unearth and throw it away. I had no craving for it all the same and I came away covering it as before. I am not the least sorry for having renounced that immense treasure. Thus through God's grace I felt neither delighted nor disgusted nor did I feel any remorse for having left it behind nor again did I entertain any craving for it. I neither brought it myself nor do I feel inclined to keep it should anyone fetch it and hand it over to me; for the Lord says: "He who renounces both good and evil is dear to Me."

"You may not covet it. I, for one, do crave for it," the woman sullenly protested. "You too should not crave for it," the Brāhmaṇa said.

× × × ×

"Ah ! There is a cobra," one of the thieves shrieked in alarm.

"The *Gītā*-lover is a great rogue", another burglar observed in a low whisper. He was convinced that the *Gītā*-lover had been philosophizing to his wife only because he had got scent of their presence in his house and that it was with the intention of having them bitten by a cobra that he had put them on the wrong scent by misrepresenting the bucket as full of diamonds and rubies.

"His wife too is no less cunning than he", a third one followed in quick succession. "The two have combined to befool us. They had really contrived to make short work of us all."

"Let us employ the same device against themselves," a fourth one suggested. "Let us throw the bucket, snake and all, into their hut and do nothing more. He will thus have mastered the formulas 'न शोचति' (he worries not) and 'न काङ्क्षति' (he craves not).

"The thieves had broken into the Brāhmaṇa's house just when he was breaking the news of the discovery of the bucket to his wife at night. And led by the report and actuated by greed they had repaired to the river-bank and unearthed the bucket; and the above conversation passed between them when they sighted the terrible cobra hissing before their very eyes as soon as they uncovered the mouth of the bucket.

All of them unanimously supported the proposal. Covering the mouth of the bucket all the four thieves lifted it on their shoulders. Getting out of breath they reached the *Gītā*-lover's house. Making a breach into the roof of the cottage, three of them slipped away. The fourth one turned the bucket upside down on the hole in the roof and took of his heels.

"Halloo ! Here is a heap of gold coins." The *Gītā*-lover's wife had been awakened by the jingling of jewels and rubies and gold coins. The snake had been crushed under the weight of the precious load. The Brāhmaṇa lady was elated with joy. "The Lord has sent us a hoard of jewels through an aperture in the roof," she said.

"You should not feel elated," the *Gītā*-lover immediately protested in an instinctive way. "God loves him alone who does not exult over the attainment of an agreeable object."

× × × ×

"We crave your forgiveness," the three brothers approached him one day and said in a spirit of humiliation.

"I harbour no ill-will against anyone, much less against you who are my own brothers. Pray don't put me to shame," the *Gītā*-lover most politely replied.

"Brother !" The voice of the three brothers was choked with emotion. They never expected such endearing words from their elder brother. One of them said, "Having parted from you we have had to suffer all along. The Goddess of Fortune has left our home for good. We have all fallen into debt. Reduced to a state of abject destitution we are leading a life of ignominy and obloquy."

"Our life has become a burden to us, brother !" Added another.

"A sense of shame prevented us from approaching you; but adversity has set spurs to us." The third one observed.

"You are our co-uterine brother," the eldest of them spoke again.

"You are a pious soul. You are giving away with open hands so much wealth to the poor everyday. We are your own brothers after all; pray forgive us," piteously observed another.

"You take these gold coins." The wailing of her three brothers-in-law had melted the *Gītā*-lover's wife. She brought a few pieces of gold and, offering them to the three brothers, said, "God has sent us this fortune by actually breaking open our roof and He will give us more."

"You should not entertain the hope that God will give us more," the Brāhmaṇa chided his wife. "It is only the desireless who stand in the good graces of the Lord."

"I crave your forgiveness for this fault." The lady acknowledged her error.

"Brother, pray allow us to reunite with you," one of the younger brothers submitted.

"Yes, brother; it will be so good of you." insisted another.

"Through your good-luck, brother, all our sufferings will come to an end," the third one also spoke in the same strain.

"He who neither rejoices nor hates, nor grieves nor desires, and who renounces both good and evil actions and is full of devotion, is dear to Me."

The *Gītā*-lover repeated the same old formula, which was his life-breath as it were, "If you want me to reunite with you, I have no objection to that; nor do I rejoice over the prospect. Even if you separate me once again, I shall not be sorry, nor shall I bear any grudge against you; for he alone who is above joy, hatred, grief and desire and renounces both good and evil, wins the favour of the Lord."

"With your very advent our house and all household goods that stood mortgaged heretofore have been released. We are free from debt now." One day, when all the four brothers met, the youngest one said, "Our life is steering smoothly these days."

"The Goddess of Fortune has turned very propitious to us," added another.

Chanting the verse 'यो न हृष्यति न द्वेष्टि' etc., the *Gītā*-lover's wife approached and said, "Come along, dear ones, the dinner is ready."

Getting ready for the dinner the third of younger brothers said, "Henceforward we too shall follow in the footsteps of our eldest brother and his wife and recite the *Gītā* regularly everyday."

"Nay, we shall try our level best to mould our life according to the *Gītā*," added the youngest.

"In that case our home will be actually transformed into a temple of God," observed yet another.

"Amen !" The *Gīta*-lover smilingly said.

[The story has been intended to depict the character of a man of retired disposition. The verse on which it has been based can be interpreted the other way as well, and thus it can very well serve as the motto of every devotee of an active disposition.]

A Sport of God, the Lover of the Devotee

(Pravīra's* wonderful Divine Love)

Pravīra was the son of Nīladhvaja, the King of Māhiṣmatī. His mother Junhādevī was an unsophisticated princess, extremely devoted to her husband as well as to virtue. In addition to Divine Love, she was possessed of exceptional self-respect, courage and patience. Her pure life exerted its complete influence on the life of Pravīra. The result was that artlessness, courtesy, love for others and Divine Love all these qualities filled his heart to the brim. Valour was reflected through every limb of his well-proportioned body, and his mind was constantly absorbed in the thought of God and Divine Love.

In those days the virtuous king Yudhiṣṭhira ruled in Indraprastha, vanquishing the Kauravas in battle on the field of Kurukṣetra. Under Bhagavān Śrī Kṛṣṇa's advice, he had decided upon performing the horse-sacrifice. The sacrificial horse had been let loose. The great archer Arjuna had been deputed to protect the horse. An army corps had been placed under his command. As the army was about to march, Bhagavān Śrī Kṛṣṇa expressed His desire to go with Arjuna. But Arjuna said, "What is the use of giving You trouble over this ordinary work ? Myself and my army are enough to conquer the whole world !" With these words, Arjuna gave the marching order to his army. Subconscious vanity and pride peeped through every line of his facial appearance.

"Anyone possessing courage to fight Arjuna may capture this horse, otherwise he is invited to attend the horse-sacrifice of

* The story of Pravīra has been dramatized in the form of a popular Yātrā current in Bengal. It is a noble and fascinating story. The present article is based on that story. Pravīra's story may be found in the Jaiminīya-Aśvamedha as well, but there it has been given in a different form.

King Yudhiṣṭhira with appropriate offerings on the appointed day"— these words of challenge were written on a plate of gold placed on the head of the horse, which proceeded as it listed, followed by a huge army commanded by Arjuna. There appeared none who could dare to lay hold of the horse. All Kings and chieftains welcomed Arjuna and accepted the overlordship of King Yudhiṣṭhira till the horse approached the town of Māhiṣmatī.

Pravīra's father, Nīladhvaja, the King of Māhiṣmatī, got frightened the moment he heard the name of Arjuna. He considered discretion to be the better part of valour, while his wife Junhādevī was roused to action at this crisis. Treating the point of view of her husband, as being prompted by cowardice, she tried hard to infuse strength in him to face Arjuna in battle in order to uphold the prestige of the Kṣatriya, but Nīladhvaja refused to be deflected from his purpose.

Disappointed with her husband, Junhādevī went to her dearest son, the great devotee Pravīra, who was the apple of her eyes, and exhorted him in the following words to fight for upholding the prestige of the Kṣatriya—"Child ! You are dearer to me than life itself, but I expect you to take your stand for the protection of the Kingdom, the nation and your own royal prestige. Arjuna's powerful army, following the sacrificial horse, is an open challenge to your Kṣatriyahood, valour, liberty and love of country. I, however, want that he may not return from this place as a conquering hero intoxicated with victory. Awake, arise, and quickly shake off your lethargy. Capture the sacrificial horse, and compel Arjuna to beat an ignominious retreat. Strike his powerful army, consisting of the four types of warriors, with your sharp arrows and do not allow it to entrench itself even for a moment."

"Mother ! Arjuna, the great hero, whose charioteer is Śrī Kṛṣṇa"!....startled Pravīra could not even complete the sentence, when like the Goddess Durgā, his beloved mother said with a roar, "Yes, he is that very Arjuna ! If you feel diffident even for a moment, speak out openly, I shall myself break through Arjuna's army and fight it single-handed. I shall console myself with the thought that I gave birth to no son at all."

"I bow my head to your order. Mother ! Please drive away your worries, and return to your quarters." Contented with this reply of Pravīra, the queen entered her quarters, and Pravīra sent his letter of challenge to Arjuna through messenger saying "I have forcibly captured your horse. Please come and free it, if you can."

The messenger brought back Arjuna's reply. Pravīra read it as follows: "O warrior ! Your letter written in the true Kṣatriya spirit has delighted my heart. I thank you sincerely for the same. But you are yet a small child. It is not proper for you to insist on entering the jaws of death, leaving aside the joys and blessings of life."

Pravīra answered immediately as follows: "O great Hero ! Words indicative of weakness do not befit you. If you are unwilling to fight, you may go back to Indraprastha. I shall never willingly release the horse."

No more parlays were necessary. The next morning, no sooner had the sun appeared on the eastern horizon, than the fight started in deadly earnest. It was a terrible fight. The sharp arrows released by the great devotee Pravīra, utterly confounded Arjuna. Addressing Pradyumna, he said, "Please cast aside the thought of Pravīra's tender youth and shower your powerful shafts upon him." But Pradyumna instantaneously replied, "Like yourself, Pravīra also is a great devotee of my father. When this thought comes to my mind, my hands become weak and I fail to exert all my strength in the fight." Thereafter, the great warrior Bhīma took his position in the front line of battle, but he also failed to make any impression against the devastating arrows of Pravīra, who had surrendered himself to the lotus-feet of God and derived all his strength from the Lord. Seeing this plight, Arjuna in great anger released the missile of fire, but the blaze of that fire was brought under complete control by strong showers of water released by Pravīra's counter-stroke of arrows. Thereafter Arjuna tried his best to cut off Pravīra's head by hurling the deadliest and most poisonous weapons he could command, but all his efforts dismally failed. Prince Pravīra by his skill and prowess confounded and vanquished the entire army of the Pāṇḍavas together with Arjuna.

Arjuna's powerful face was darkened by the cloud of despair and sorrow. At that moment Pravīra came forward and said, "Hero, Arjuna ! Is this the force depending on which you released the sacrificial horse ! Please take this clear warning from me, if life is not dear to you, you may challenge me, again, tomorrow for the fight. Otherwise I give you leave to retire in peace with my invitation to come here with your offerings when I perform sacrifice with this very horse. Without the help of Bhagavān Śrī Kṛṣṇa you can never expect to vanquish me. If you intend to conquer me, summon Śrī Kṛṣṇa to your aid, so that by His sight my innermost desire may be fulfilled." As he uttered these words, Pravīra's mind got wholly absorbed in the meditation of Śrī Kṛṣṇa.

The above words of Pravīra, like powerful shafts, pierced Arjuna's heart. He now realized the error of bragging before the Lord: "O Hari ! O Lord ! O Govinda ! O Vāsudeva ! O Nārāyaṇa ! Please forgive me for uttering those impertinent words. You are Omniscient, Almighty, and the Supreme Lord. Please appear soon and give me Your kind protection." The moment Arjuna's cry of distress reached Him, the Lord who is the remover of the fear of the devotee, at once manifested Himself there, as if He had remained hidden somewhere near about the place.

At the sight of the Lord, Arjuna fell prostrate at His feet. When the Lord turned His face, He observed Pravīra also offering obeisance, falling like a piece of log on the ground. The Lord met both the devotees. Pravīra's delight knew no bounds. Through excess of joy, he exclaimed, "Lord ! I feel quite blessed, indeed, at Your sight." Then, turning towards Arjuna, he said, "Pārtha ! I am deeply indebted to you as well; for it was through your grace that I enjoy the privilege of this sweet and fascinating sight of our beloved Lord, which purifies the three worlds. I am now going back to my camp. From tomorrow, we shall fight in the very presence of the Lord." Thus both the warriors retired to their respective camps.

The moment Pravīra's mother, Junhādevī, met her heroic son, she pressed him to her bosom, and said, "Child ! I am going to worship the Goddess Gaṅgā for your victory." Pravīra's devoted wife, Madanamañjarī, expressing great delight, said, "I shall propitiate Bhagavān Śrī Kṛṣṇa by my devotion and pray to Him for your victory." Pravīra himself was all the while absorbed in meditation on the Lord.

It was past midnight, when Pravīra's wife, Madanamañjarī, passed through the lines of Arjuna's armed camp lulled to sleep. She carried a long sword in her hand, unsheathed from the scabbard. Lord Śaṅkara stood on guard at the camp with His trident in hand. He challenged Madanamañjarī and asked her about the cause of her entering the camp at that hour, with a drawn sword in her hand.

Madanamañjarī told Him the whole truth without any reserve. "I am Pravīra's wife", she said, "I have entered this camp in order to meet Bhagavān Śrī Kṛṣṇa for the protection of my husband's life."

Bhagavān Śaṅkara replied, "This is not possible. Śrī Kṛṣṇa has now retired to bed. Please go back to your own place."

"If that is so, here is my head which I shall throw at your

feet"—saying this Madanamañjarī raised her sword.

Then, revealing who He was, Bhagavān Śaṅkara said, "I am extremely pleased with you, and am going back to Kailāsa. My responsibility ceases when I leave this place."

When Madanamañjarī reached the very door of Śrī Kṛṣṇa's tent, she was again challenged by the sentry standing guard there. But there, also, she said, "I am the daughter-in-law of. King Nīladhvaja seeking interview with Bhagavān Śrī Kṛṣṇa for begging the life of my beloved husband."

The sentry replied, "Go hence. The Lord has now retired to bed."

Drawing her sword, Madanamañjarī said again "If you do not allow me to go to the Lord, I shall throw my head as an offering at your feet."

The sentry caught hold of Madanamañjarī's hand, when she discovered that He was none else than Bhagavān Śrī Kṛṣṇa, the Lord of the three worlds, the Enchanter of Cupid himself, to meet whom she had come risking her very life. She at once fell at the Lord's feet. Then, after a spell of silence, she humbly submitted: "Lord ! You are the knower of hearts. Yet I cannot restrain myself from making this humble submission. When the day will break, there will be a fight between the great archer Arjuna and my beloved husband. Arjuna is assisted by You; with Your help he is capable of doing whatever he likes, therefore, I beg the life of my husband from You."

Giving to her His own powerful club, named Kaumodakī, and His own discus Sudarśana, the Lord who is the friend of the devotee and the embodiment of mercy, told, her, "Look here ! So long as Pravīra keeps these weapons with him, none will be able to kill him in battle." Bowing her head to the Lord's feet, Madanamañjarī quickly retraced her steps and delivered the two weapons to her husband. She also reported to him what the Lord had said with regard to them.

Pravīra's mother, Junhādevī, on her part, had propitiated the Goddess Gaṅgā and prayed to her to request her husband, Śiva, to fight on Pravīra's side. But no sooner had He heard the request, than Śiva said that Arjuna was assisted by Śrī Kṛṣṇa and that it was impossible for Him to take side in a battle as an adversary of Śrī Kṛṣṇa.

With the break of dawn Arjuna went to see his bosom friend and found Him seated with downcast look, merged in anxiety and deep thought. Observing Arjuna, Śrī Kṛṣṇa said, "Friend ! Pleased with the devotion of Pravīra's wife, I have given away both my weapons to her. So long as she possesses those weapons, none can do any injury to her. My presence near you invariably creates only obstacles in your path."

The words of the Lord angered Bhīma, the second Pāṇḍava. He said, "You ought to have granted the boon after some thought and reflection. Have You come for our protection, or for increasing the burden of our difficulties ?" When, however, Bhīma closed his lips, Arjuna with full faith and great humility observed: "What do You say, my Lord ? I strongly believe that there is some blessing hidden behind every act of Yours. This gift made by You of Your weapons also involves some good to me. I do not entertain the least anxiety on this account. You are all-in-all to us. It is You who inspired us to undertake this horse-sacrifice and gave us assurance about its success. Now, please do whatever You consider best for us."

Bhagavān Śrī Kṛṣṇa kept silent. He was anxious for Arjuna, who wholly depended on Him, and could not say anything. Arjuna, however, broke the oppressive silence. He said, "Lord ! It is already dawn. We should now get ready for the fight. Please give us Your command."

Śrī Kṛṣṇa replied, "Come, let us go to Śaṅkara. He may give us some good advice to meet this difficulty." The moment they formed this intent, both of them reached the abode of Śaṅkara.

There, addressing Śaṅkara, Śrī Kṛṣṇa said, "Lord ! Pleased with the devotion of Pravīra's wife, I gave away my club as well as my discus for the sake of her husband. So long as they are in Pravīra's possession, nobody can expect to kill him in battle. We have therefore, come to learn from You how Arjuna may attain victory in this battle."

Śrī Śaṅkara said, "Omniscient as You are, how did You grant the boon to her ?" Śrī Kṛṣṇa replied, "Just as delighted with the intensity of her devotion, You left for Kailāsa that very night, even so I had to grant the boon charmed by her devotion."

In slow accents, Bhagavān Śaṅkara said, "I really find myself face to face with a great dilemma. On the one hand, pleased with the worship of Pravīra's mother. Śrī Gaṅgā is pressing Me hard to take the side of Pravīra and fight Arjuna with My trident in hand; and, on the other, stands Your request. I have, therefore, decided not to enter the battlefield on behalf of any party whatsoever."

In a tone full of despair, Śrī Kṛṣṇa, then, said to Arjuna, "Brother ! This was, indeed, My last and final resort, but He has given us a straight, cold reply. What should we do next ?" Arjuna replied, "Lord ! I know nothing about these means. What I know is only this, that whatever You do will certainly lead to my good. The time of joining the battle is fast approaching."

Reflecting a little, the next moment Śrī Kṛṣṇa went to see Goddess Umā, accompanied by Arjuna. There He described to the Goddess all facts about Yudhiṣṭhira's undertaking the horse-sacrifice, Pravīra's opposition to the same, the gift made by Him of His own weapons and the boon granted by Him and prayed for Arjuna's victory, requesting the Goddess to assume an enchanting form and deprive Pravīra of those weapons. The Goddess Umā agreed to do this. Finding that His mission had become successful, Śrī Kṛṣṇa quickly returned to the camp with Arjuna.

Entering the battleground, Arjuna saw that Pravīra had been waiting for him with his powerful army. As the battle was about to start, Pravīra saw before him in the sky the vision of a young woman of enchanting form and incomparable beauty. He could never imagine that there could be such loveliness in the whole universe. God's power of illusion, which is capable of bringing to pass what is otherwise impossible, wholly brought under its spell the mind of the devotee, Pravīra, who had full control over her passion, and like an ordinary lustful person, he began to crave for his love. Such is the power of Māyā.

The Goddess in that extremely lovely form said, "Overtures of love in the field of battle sound like incoherent talk. If you are really sincere in your desire for return of love, throw away those two weapons of yours." Held under the spell of Māyā, Pravīra had lost all power of thought. He threw away both the weapons given to him by Lord Śrī Kṛṣṅa. Quickly picking them up from the ground, the Goddess disappeared from the scene. The veil of Māyā was then lifted. When the truth at last dawned on Pravīra, he began to repent, muttering within himself, "What a sin have I committed today !"

Finally he thought that the hand of God must be behind all that had happened. Therefore, lovingly expressing his anger, he said, "Lord ! If it was Your intention to deprive me of those weapons with the help of Your illusive power, what was the purpose of Your giving them to me at all ?" The Lord replied, "Pravīra, dear, I did not take away those weapons from you. Had it been My desire to take them away, why should I give them to you ?" Pravīra quickly rejoined, "Lord ! If that is so, You should not lend Your support to Arjuna in the present conflict. I also regard You as dearer than life itself. My devotion to You is in no sense inferior to that of Arjuna."

Hearing those words of Pravīra, Arjuna said, "Lord ! I invited You to come here to help me in the battle. If Pravīra feels himself powerless, let him release the sacrificial horse." But Pravīra angrily retorted, "I did not capture the horse in order to release it." Thereafter no more words were wasted—and both the sides engaged themselves in a mortal combat. The sky was overcast with the arrows of the rival armies—but all the skill possessed by Arjuna was baffled, and he began gradually to yield ground to his adversary.

The Lord said, "Arjuna ! See the power of the devotee. Although I am helping you in the fight, yet he is defeating you." Showering arrows from his bow without any break, Arjuna replied, "Lord ! That is why I have invited You to come and help me. Through Your grace, I shall now vanquish him in a trice."

Arjuna aimed and released a sharp arrow, but Pravīra cut it into several parts before it traversed even half the distance. Whatever weapon Arjuna hurled was destroyed by Pravīra, but in the end that day's fight went in favour of Arjuna.

Thereupon Pravīra angrily said, "Arjuna ! I do not regard this victory as yours, but it is the Lord's victory. I shall recognize you as a hero, if you can vanquish me without the help of the Lord." Arjuna replied, "When I have invited the Lord to help me, why should I ignore His help ? If you are afraid to fight, you may retire from the field of battle."

Hearing these words of Arjuna, the devotee Pravīra, addressing the Lord, said, "O my Beloved Lord ! You belong to all, why should You then show this partiality in the field of battle ?" In the form of reply, he saw the smile of the Lord, which bewitches the entire universe. Why should he wait any more ? Observing the Lord pleased with him, Pravīra held Him by the hand and pulling Him by force brought Him to his own chariot. The Lord took up the reins of his horses. Full of confidence, Pravīra said, "Arjuna ! You may now fight to your heart's content. You will either have to run away with your life, or take to eternal sleep."

Instead of giving any direct answer to Pravīra, Arjuna prayed to the Lord: 'O Lord ! I cannot live without You. Please return to my chariot. You came here at my invitation." The Lord thereupon came to Arjuna's chariot and held the reins of the horses.

Depressed in spirit, Pravīra said, "Lord ! Could You not drive my chariot for the duration of at least a single fight ?" Then, addressing Arjuna, he said, "Today, I shall test your manliness."

Arjuna was showering sharp arrows through his bow with very great care, but Pravīra was no ordinary warrior. Arjuna, therefore, could not keep his hands steady. This made the Lord exclaim in surprise, "Although you have got my full assistance, Arjuna, yet you are not gaining victory !" Hurling a powerful weapon of fire, Arjuna replied, "Keep patience for a little while, Lord, I shall presently defeat the enemy."

But his attempts continued to fail. In the end, with the help of some supernatural weapons Pravīra was vanquished on that day, for which rebuking Arjuna, Pravīra said, "One fighting on the strength of another cannot be called a hero. Without the help of the Lord, you do not possess any power by means of which you can expect to defeat me in battle."

Then, addressing the Lord, he said "Lord ! You belong equally to both of us. Please give up now this work of driving Arjuna's chariot, and see our respective skill of war as an impartial spectator. Then, You will really know who, as between the two of us, is the better warrior, and Arjuna on his part also will get the taste of a battle."

The Lord smiled at his words. The devotee, Pravīra, finding the Lord pleased with him, again, pulled Him out of Arjuna's chariot and tied Him to an adjoining palm tree. Then, addressing Arjuna, he said, "Now Arjuna, come and give a demonstration of your skill in battle before me. I shall make you taste the bitter fruit of a contest with me." Looking at the Lord with a pitiable look in his eyes Arjuna, however, said, "O Lord ! Did I invite You to come here to show me this sight ? When the powerful warriors in the Kaurava Court had failed to hold You in bondage, how did You submit today to be tied up by an ordinary rope ? I feel quite confounded, Lord ! Please come to me soon and take charge of the reins of my chariot." God, the possessor of inconceivable power, whose one single Name liberates one from bondage, came today under the bondage of the rope in the form of Love of one of His loving devotees. On the other side stands an equally great devotee whose words of utter humility is also drawing the Lord towards him. As soon as He heard Arjuna's cry of distress, the Lord broke the rope that tied Him to the tree and getting into Arjuna's chariot began to drive it as before. He found Himself in a peculiar predicament today. Pulled by two loving devotees in two opposite directions, He was playing a wonderful part, becoming the very embodiment of Love Himself.

Pravīra could not restrain himself. Addressing the Lord, he, again, said, "Lord ! What a matter of surprise ! Could You not stand as an impartial spectator even for a little while, and see the fight and heroism of two of Your contesting devotees ? But let Your will be done." Then turning towards Arjuna, he said, "You have not the least heroism in you. The effort to vanquish a competing hero in a field of battle with another's help cannot be too strongly condemned." In great fury he showered so many sharp arrows and supernatural weapons that Arjuna lost control over himself and his entire army fearfully mauled and bruised dispersed like a rabble. Here, also, it was the sport of God that was operating.

Expressing surprise at this sight of debacle, Bhagavān Śrī Kṛṣṇa said, "When Pravīra single-handed has reduced you to this state, what impression can you expect to make on the other warriors ?" Arjuna rallied his broken army and encouraged it to join the fight again reminding all warriors about the bright fate of those participating in a righteous war. The huge army reformed itself and attacked the army of Pravīra with all its might. Arjuna, on his part began to shower arrows with unprecedented valour. Both sides employed their full power for the attainment of victory. In the end, Pravīra was defeated this day, and the honour of victory went to Arjuna.

But Pravīra, the great hero, had not the least worry on this account. He, again, rebuked Arjuna, saying, "Arjuna ! Adopt the quality of a true hero. If you fight without the assistance of Śrī Kṛṣṇa, I think it will be difficult for you to save your life." And turning towards Śrī Kṛṣṇa, he said, "Lord ! I am also Your humble devotee, but I find that You make differentiation between Arjuna and me. Why do You do so, Lord ! I entertain great hopes from You."

The Lord smiled at his words. Regarding the Lord favourable towards him Pravīra again pulled the Lord by the hand, and tied him strongly for the second time to an adjoining palm tree, and said, "Lord ! This time please give me Your promise that instead of taking any side You will see the fight as a neutral observer." Smilingly the Lord gave His silent consent to the proposal.

What more was to be expected ? Quickly leaping into his chariot, Pravīra took up his bow and arrow, and, challenging Arjuna, said, "Pārtha ! Be prepared now either to run away from the field or to embrace eternal sleep. The Lord has given me promise." Tied down to the tree, the Lord was smiling at these words, as if He was enjoying the state of compulsion to which He had been subjected by Pravīra.

But Arjuna's eyes were fixed on the Lord. He said, "What play are You playing, my Lord ! It has now placed my very life in danger. I am utterly perplexed. During the war with the Kauravas You had promised not to take up arms for my protection, but for the sake of Your devotee You had to break it. That very beloved Arjuna of Yours is today going to embrace death, hence break Your promise again and protect me by coming to my aid soon." Immediately the Lord manifested Himself in the war-chariot of Arjuna. He appeared smiling there just as He had been smiling a little while before.

Taken aback at this sight, Pravīra said, "Lord ! What have You done ? Have You not broken Your own word of honour ?" At once the Lord replied, "I did not bind Myself with any promise."

Expressing his affectionate anger, the devotee Pravīra retorted, "Lord ! If you also take to the utterance of untruth, what will be the fate of this unhappy world ? You gave me promise that You would quietly see the fight as a neutral observer, but I find You now occupying the seat of the driver in Arjuna's chariot."

The Lord replied, "Brother ! Tell this to Him, who gave you this promise." Turning back to the palm tree, Pravīra observed that the Lord stood there tied to the tree as before. He began to turn his gaze once towards the palm tree, and again in the direction of Arjuna's chariot. He found that the same Lord had assumed two forms. Thereupon, addressing Arjuna, Pravīra said, "Arjuna ! You are indeed, a blessed soul ! Your parents, who have brought you to this earth, are also blessed; for your sake, the Lord had to assume these two forms today."

Pravīra fixed his gaze on both the forms of the Lord. The ocean of Love within him began to rise and swell as if under the influence of a flood. He totally forgot himself. The supernatural loveliness of the Lord's eternally new form, which stupefies the mind of even gods and sages, created such a magic influence on Pravīra that he wholly lost consciousness of the external world. He got absolutely merged in that supernatural ocean of sweetness of the Lord's nectarean form.

At this stage, the Lord commanded, "Arjuna ! Quickly cut off Pravīra's head." But Arjuna replied, "Lord ! Pravīra has given up the fight, and is absorbed in Your meditation; it is contrary to the laws of battle to kill him in this state."

The Lord quickly retorted, "Arjuna ! Who is there on earth who can kill My devotee Pravīra, in a direct fight with him ? My intention is that My devotee should go to My Supreme Abode absorbed in meditation on Me. My command is that you should now put him to death. If you carry this out, you will remain untouched by sin."

Arjuna released a very sharp supernatural shaft possessing the shape of the crescent moon, which separated Pravīra's head from his body, and the head thereupon suddenly bounded up and dropped at Śrī Kṛṣṇa's feet. A bright lustre coming out of Pravīra's body merged in the blessed form of the Lord. With Pravīra's death the remnant of his army scattered on all sides. The whole of Māhiṣmatī was plunged in grief.

Hearing the news of Pravīra's death, his father began to lament for him and his weeping mother, feeling proud for the heroic end of her son, worthy of a great devotee, said, "Child ! You have entered the Lord's abode, falling in battle against Arjuna, which has proved me to be the mother of a true Kṣatriya hero. My life's object has been fulfilled."

When they were thus lamenting the death of Pravīra, the Lord entered Māhiṣmatī and went up to them. Addressing the weeping mother, Junhādevī, He said, "Please do not worry over what has taken place. If you so desire, I shall bring back Pravīra to life." Junhādevī replied, "Lord ! Attaining death before You, who will seek to come back to life again ? My humble prayer is that You may kindly grant us the high state which You granted to our fortunate son."

"So be it", said the Lord, and thereafter He further directed: "King Nīladhvaja should now give a respectful and friendly farewell to Arjuna, and then at the appointed time he should attend the horse-sacrifice of King Yudhiṣṭhira with proper offerings, where he will again see Me." Uttering these words, the Lord disappeared from the scene.

As directed by the Lord, Nīladhvaja offered a most courteous and respectful farewell to Arjuna and thereafter he completely merged himself in the Bhajana of the Lord. The devoted wife of Pravīra, Madanamañjarī, on her part, offering herself as a Satī, attained the Supreme Abode of the Lord.

How to Develop Love for God and Faith in Saints ?

God, as a matter of fact, is the only object worthy of love. As regards saints they call for more of our reverence than love. God, however, claims both inasmuch as He is transcendental, ethereal and spiritual in substance. The body of a saint, on the other hand, is material, physical. The very sight of the Lord bestows beatitude; but such is not the case with a saint. Mere attachment or love for the physical body of a saint cannot ensure final redemption. What is required, therefore, is faith in him. What does faith denote ? In short, faith consists in doing the bidding of a saint. One cannot be sure of one's redemption through mere bodily service of a saint or through worship offered to his physical frame. On the other hand, one is sure to attain liberation by carrying out the behests of a saint. Service rendered or worship offered to a saint will only make him ease-loving. That is the reason why saints generally do not accept any service or homage. They shun physical comforts as well as honour and praise.

One can be redeemed by developing love even for God's essential character, pastimes, divine Abode, Name or virtues. Hence God deserves our love. Love for anything other than God is risky. One should have faith in the scriptures, the other world, a saint and God; all of them deserve our faith. But no other object than God deserves our love. We spend most of our time with the object of our love. We cannot be redeemed even if we live with a saint for fifty years but never care to carry out his instructions. Both his example and precepts are conducive to blessedness. Pertaining to this the *Gītā* says:—

"For whatever a great man does, that very thing other men also do; whatever standard he sets up, the generality of men follows the same" (III.21).

"Other dull-witted persons, however, not knowing thus, worship even as they have heard from others; and even those who are devoted to hearing, are able to cross the ocean of mundane existence in the shape of death." (XIII.25).

Listening attentively to the words of a saint, they who abide by his advice and strive accordingly are able to cross the ocean of worldly existence, devoted as they are to the process of hearing. How can one get devoted by hearing ? Take the example of a deer who listens to the music of a flute and gets so enraptured with it that he is practically lost to the outer world and would offer little resistence even if you entrap it or even kill it. Similarly, one should drink in each and every word of a saint with rapt attention. One should then try to follow what one has heard and carry it into practice. There are many who listen to the discourse of a saint; but one is benefited only when one assimilates and translates his words into practice. Our inability to retain what we have heard is attributable to lack of faith. He who after listening to the words of a scripture of a saint puts implicit faith in them, and makes up his mind to abide by them even at the cost of his life, attains blessedness. "Even death in the performance of one's own duty brings blessedness" (III.35), says the *Gītā*. Therefore, the *sine qua non* of blessedness is faith. The greater our faith, the speedier is the success. This is corroborated by the *Gītā*, which says:—"He who has mastered his senses, is exclusively devoted to his practice and is full of faith attains enlightenment; having had the revelation of Truth, he immediately attains supreme peace (in the form of God-Realization)" (IV.39).

A man of faith attains wisdom. What is a man of faith like ? He is steadfast in his spiritual practice. Why was it necessary to qualify the word 'Śraddhāvān' with the use of the adjective 'Tatparaḥ' ? Because the degree of earnestness one evinces in one's Sādhanā (spiritual discipline) bespeaks the amount of faith one possesses. The earnestness of one's striving is the criterion of one's Śraddhā (faith). Even as a greedy man directs all his energies towards an object which is conducive to his gain and spares no pains to achieve it, a seeker of blessedness allows no laxity in his spiritual practice once he gets fully convinced that by following a particular practice he will attain blessedness. A man imbued with faith attains spiritual enlightenment and from spiritual enlightenment follows supreme peace; but where earnestness is absent faith is lacking. The Lord uses one more qualifying word 'Saṁyatendriyaḥ', *i.e.,* he who has mastered his senses. The man who has not his mind and senses under control is not prosecuting his spiritual practice in right earnest. Lack of faith has its root in ignorance.

When the hour of death arrives, it cannot be deferred even for a moment by offering lakhs of rupees, no amount of wailing or intercession proves of any avail. Such being the case, it should be our bounded duty not to rest contented till we have succeeded in attaining God-Realization. We should not allow ourselves time even to talk with others. Who knows in what species of life we may be reborn in case our Sādhanā falls short of its consummation even slightly and we have to depart from this world without realizing God. All species of life other than the human life are meant for pleasurable and painful experiences as a result of past actions. In the human species alone God can be easily realized; then why should we look forward to any subsequent birth ? On the other hand, we should achieve our object in this very birth; otherwise there is great risk for us.

In a certain village there lived a saint of a high order. People used to visit him frequently. The news reached the king of the realm too. Urged by the people of that village he too paid a visit to him one day. The saint had already come to know that the king was very lascivious and voluptuous and had concluded that if the latter came round the people too would be benefited alongwith him. So when the king arrived the saint enquired of his welfare. The king implored him to give him some tonic which might enable him to copulate with any number of women without being exhausted. At this the saint called for a bottle from his cottage. He gave two drops of its contents to the king to swallow and the rest he himself drank off. The king returned to his palace, and at night he satisfied all his queens when he felt the sexual urge; yet the passion in him knew no appeasement. His urge continued unabated. Three days hence he renewed his visit to the saint and said, "Your aphrodisiac works wonders; pray, give me two more drops." The saint gave him the dose. In this way he took two drops from the saint every third day for two or three months and revelled in sexual enjoyment. Each time the saint himself quaffed the rest of it in the presence of the king. One day the king came and asked the saint to give him some drug which might obviate the necessity of approaching and bothering him again and again and which might prove effectual for the whole of his life. At this the saint gave him a full bottle to drink, which the king gladly did. When he had finished the bottle, the saint regretfully remarked that he had made a grievous blunder. "What mistake have you committed ?" the king enquired. The saint after much hesitation told him that he would die after an interval of three days. The king wondered if what he said was true whereupon the saint endorsed his remark. Asked by the king whether there was anyway of escape, the saint after much deliberation observed that there was no doubt a way but that it was a herculean task. With all eagerness the king expressed his willingness to undertake the work however difficult it might be, and enquired about the same. "From this time onward till the last moment of your life, pray, forget not the Divine Name !" commanded the saint. The king agreed and made up his mind to act accordingly. Returning to his palace he retired to a lonely apartment and sat there all alone. He got it proclaimed by beat of drum that nobody should visit him and that anyone who contravened his order would receive capital punishment. He got so deeply absorbed in his devotions and meditation that he forget all about himself and thought no more of food, drink or even of evacuating his bowels or bladder. As a result of continued meditation on God his egosense died and he passed into an unbroken state of Samādhi (trance). Seven days rolled by, but his Samādhi did not break. Now the people outside wondered that the king was to die on the fourth day but that there was no news about him even though seven days had elapsed. They went inside and found the king in a state of trance. The din and bustle at last broke the king's Samādhi. The king called for an explanation as to why the doors of his room had been opened before the expiry of three days. People told him that seven days had elapsed. The king now recalled the words of the saint who had told him that he would die after three days, and wondered how it had not happened. With this doubt lurking in his mind he approached the saint once again and told him the whole episode. The saint enquired whether the "I" was still left in him. The king replied in the negative. The saint now explained to him that the "I" or the ego in him had died, while there was no question of his physical death yet. The king further expressed his wonder at the fact that the saint drank away a whole bottle of the tonic everyday, yet it did not have any effect on him; whereas even two drops of it had an astounding effect on the king. The saint replied that only seven days before the king too had taken a full bottle of it yet it did not have any effect on him either. The king then told the saint how he thought neither of his wives nor of his progeny during the whole week inasmuch as he saw death imminent. The saint corroborated the king's experience and added that in his own case, he saw death staring him in the face every moment, hence the tonic could have no effect on him.

Even as the king, though exceedingly libidinous, attained blessedness within seven days because of his earnestness, we too can likewise reach that state in a comparatively short time if only we feel death knocking at our door.

The cause of the king's earnestness was his conviction that death would snatch away his life just after three days. Hence he gave up eating and drinking and like Dhruva got completely immersed in meditation. Similarly we can also speedily realize that blissful state if we visualize death as imminent and considering every second as invaluable devote ourselves to meditation day and night. Time is very short, it should be regarded as most precious. If we fail to attain blessedness now there is great risk ahead of us. Other than God there is no one to protect us. If we lose this opportunity we shall meet our doom like a parentless child. Thus visualizing death as near at hand we should get completely immersed in the thought of God—herein lies our welfare.

Question: Is there any possibility of redemption even for a man lacking intelligence, discretion and knowledge ?

Answer: Yes, if he cultivates the fellowship of saints and follows their directions, pursues a course of discipline recommended by them.

Question: Suppose a man awakes at the eleventh hour, when death has drawn very near, can he be redeemed or not ?

Answer: Yes, he can be saved even like the king in the above anecdote. The highest degree of earnestness can bring about one's redemption quickly.

Question: Is there any hope for redemption of a person who is highly immoral, libidinous, sensual and addicted to vices ?

Answer: Yes, he can be redeemed very quickly as was the case with the king referred to above. The Lord Himself avers it when He says:—

"Even if the vilest sinner worships Me with exclusive devotion, he should be accounted a saint; for he has rightly resolved (He is positive in his belief that there is nothing like devoted worship of God)."

"Speedily he becomes virtuous and secures lasting peace. Know it for certain, Arjuna, that My devotee never falls."

"Arjuna women, Vaiśyas (members of the trading and agriculturist classes), Śūdras (those belonging to the labouring and artisan classes), as well as those of vile birth (such as the Pariah), whoever they may be, taking refuge in Me they too attain the supreme goal" (Gītā IX.30—32).

There is hope even for the most sinful. Of course his mind must be undivided. He must devote himself exclusively to the worship of God as the king in the above parable. One's devotion must be exclusive, as that of Prahlāda, or of a faithful wife who is exclusively devoted to her husband. One must not seek anything else than God. His fidelity must be undivided. God alone must be the object of his constant worship. Such a man speedily turns into a saint. There is no delay for him. Only his devotion must be exclusive and uninterrupted. When even such great sinners are redeemed there can be no doubt about the redemption of virtuous souls. It is equally true that there is no liberation without spiritual enlightenment; but it can be secured by divine grace. The man who is engaged in constant worship is blessed with such enlightenment by God; the Lord Himself says:—

"On those ever united through meditation with Me and worshipping Me with love, I confer that Yoga of wisdom through which they come to Me" (Gītā X.10).

The *Gītā* reveals the exalted glory of those who are engaged in constant remembrance of God. Thus proclaims the Lord:—

"These, Arjuna, I speedily deliver from the ocean of birth and death, their mind being fixed on Me" (Gītā XII.7).

Then follows His exhortation—

"Fix your mind on Me, and establish your intellect in Me alone; thereafter you will abide solely in Me. There is no doubt about it" (*Gītā* XII.8).

From this it follows that impressed with the exclusive devotion of His worshipper, the Lord blesses him with spiritual enlightenment however ignorant he may be. Even the vilest sinner is redeemed by virtue of his devotion. A man is redeemed through Devotion however near his death may be. Devotion to God is possible only when we love Him; we develop love for Him only through Devotion. The two are interdependent. Realizing this and regarding death as quite imminent and time as most valuable, one should apply oneself to Devotion heart and soul. Let us not forget God even for a moment. For not a second can be added to our allotted span of life even if we spend a lakh of rupees. No amount of wailing or recommendations would then avail. When the destined hour comes you must quit the world at all events. In no way can one's life be prolonged even for a couple of hours. And death may come any moment, there is no certainty about it. For whenever it comes it comes by surprise; it gives you no previous notice. Hence one should not make any calculation about death and should be ever ready to face it. If you have escaped it today you may not be spared tomorrow; and if you survive tomorrow there is little hope of your being spared the next day. Thinking like this one should exert oneself for God-Realization. Let us take a vow either to attain God this very day or to die. Spurning all other duties we must give priority to this work. For, if we depart from this world today, we shall have no more connection with our wealth, family, progeny and lordship than our father and grandfather. We do not remember today anything concerning our past life as to where we resided, what we were, what was our rank and position in society and what power we enjoyed. Similarly we shall forget everything about our present life in our next birth. Therefore, it will be sheer stupidity on our part to fritter away our time in amassing worldly riches etc. Although we wasted our time in our previous births let us not waste it over these things at least in this life. To say nothing of our worldly possessions, even this body would not accompany us after death. Realizing this fact one should cease to have any infatuation for anything belonging to this world. That body alone is ours which helps us in redeeming our soul. That wealth alone is ours which helps us in attaining blessedness. That son alone is ours who helps us in securing liberation. And that fortune alone should be accounted ours, which helps us in reaching the ultimate goal of life; otherwise it is only misfortune for us. Pondering this one should gird up oneself to realize the object of one's existence. Why should we claim this body as ours when it is bound to part from us one day ? If it is going to drop tomorrow, let it drop this very day. As a matter of fact, we shall die only when we are to die. There is also a story illustrating this fact too:—

There was a man hailing from Rajasthan, who lived outside. He went home with his family after twenty years. His house had remained closed all these years. He unlocked it and had it cleaned of dirt etc. At night when they all retired a number of ghosts appeared and asked them to clear off. The owner of the house, however, claimed the house as his own and declined to go. The ghosts in their turn insisted that the house had been in their possession and asked him to quit it. The owner then asked their leave to sleep there overnight and promised to vacate the premises the following day. The next night also the family slept there, and again the ghosts appeared and demanded that they should leave the house. The owner of the house requested them to bear with them for a few days more, promising to evacuate the premises as soon as they had arranged to get another house for themselves. He thus went on equivocating for some time till one night the owner of the house enquired of the ghosts as to which place they resorted to during the day-time. The ghosts told him that they went to and remained with King Yama (the god of death) during the day, thereupon the owner of the house entreated them to do him a favour by ascertaining from Yama as to how long he and his people were destined to live. The ghosts agreed to do this. The following night when the ghosts returned, they on enquiry told him the allotted span of life of all the members of his family, which was different in each case. But the owner of the house did not rest there. He asked one more favour of the ghosts. "Since King Yama is your friend, pray, request him on my behalf either to prolong or to reduce the span of life of everyone of us by one day. They treated this request of his as most simple and assured him that it would be granted. When, however, they approached Yama and conveyed to him the request of the owner of their house, King Yama pleaded his helplessness in the matter, adding that the allotted span of life of any individual whatsoever did not admit of the slightest alteration either way. The ghosts then returned and repeated to him every word of what Yama had told them. When the ghosts pressed him again to quit the house he prevaricated as before. The ghosts grew indignant this time and threatened to take his life if he failed to leave the premises. The owner of the house now mustered courage and said, "Pooh, what power have you to deliver us to death before our time, when even Yama is powerless to do so ?" The bold stand taken by the owner of that house brought the ghosts to their senses and they quietly left the house themselves. Hence we need not worry about our end. 'Every bullet has its billet,' goes the proverb. We shall die only when the time comes, neither a day sooner nor a day later. Therefore one need not exert oneself to have one's life prolonged. On the other hand, we should try our best to redeem our soul so long as we live on earth. Beware lest death should pounce on you before you have attained blessedness and leave you no choice but to repent. Gosvāmī Tulasīdāsa says well:— "He reaps torture in the other world and beats his head in remorse, wrongly attributing the blame to Time, Fate and God." Therefore, if we fail to attain our goal even though blessed with a human body, we shall rue it. Over and above the privilege of a human body granted to us we are being repeatedly warned by the Lord Himself, the Vedas and the Smṛti texts as well as by God-realized saints like Kabīra and Tulasīdāsa.

Kabīra says:—

"Kabīra ! The tabor and trumpet for the nonce, you may play;
You won't see again.
This township and market gay !"

Similarly, the Lord exhorts us in the *Gītā* as follows—

"Having obtained this joyless and transient human life, constantly worship Me."

He further says:—

"Fix your mind on Me, be devoted to Me, worship Me and make obeisance to Me; thus linking yourself with Me and entirely depending on Me, you shall come to Me" (Gītā IX. 34).

You have been hearing all these precepts for the past several years. But in few cases, that I know of, the progress made has reached the desired level. You and I had a number of friends—some rich and others poor; but they have all left us. Our seniors in age have gone; those of our own age have also departed and our juniors too have left us. We shall also follow suit. We cognize this with the help of our reason and the scriptures too enlighten us; but it still remains an enigma to us. While replying to the questions of Dharma disguised as a Yakṣa, Yudhiṣṭhira too makes a similar statement in the *Mahābhārata:—*

"We find living beings flocking to the abode of Death everyday; yet those who remain behind expect to survive till eternity. Can there be a greater wonder than this ?"

We try to impress this truth upon multitudes of men and caution our own friends; yet some people would put off things till their debts have been cleared off. Others promise to take to adoration with a tranquil mind only after their sons have been married. A third one has the consolation that everything else is all right, that his sons too are clever; but the only affair that remains to be settled by him is the question of income-tax. Such is the condition of our friends. Many of them have passed away and the rest will surely follow suit; but there appears none who may be said to have provided himself against death. That is why we ask everyone to take to spiritual practice inasmuch as the time at our disposal is very short. People agree to do this and give us an assurance to that effect. Many of them have breathed their last while making such vain promises. Now whom shall we exhort and how ? They would not understand while they are alive and we have no means to exhort them once they have departed. People who remained engrossed in the thought of their family and wealth eventually died with the same thought foremost in their mind. Neither did their worries leave them nor could they redeem their soul. We still repeat the same advice to many, but without any appreciable result. Either we are to blame for this or those who hear our discourses. Surely it is no fault of God, who is extremely compassionate. His grace is ever flowing in an unending stream; it is so abundant that it transcends all our conception. The Lord Himself says:—

"Having known Me as the disinterested friend of all beings, My devotee attains peace" (*Gītā* V.29).

God is disinterestedly merciful. This is corroborated even by Lord Śiva in the *Rāmacaritamānasa*. He says:—

"Umā, there is no such well-wisher as Śrī Rāma in this world—neither preceptor, nor father, nor mother, nor brother, nor master."

This human body has been vouchsafed to us by God in His

great mercy. The *Rāmacaritamānasa says:—*

"Rarely does God, who loves the Jīva without any self-interest, graciously bestow on it a human form."

In this way taking every occurrence as a propitious dispensation of God, we should feel supremely contented and rejoice. We should feel His compassion pervading everywhere and know Him to be our supreme well-wisher. Who is there so rich and so compassionate as He ? When we take refuge in Him we shall attain supreme tranquillity. Let us treat every joy and sorrow that comes to us unexpected and uncalled for as his benign will. By developing such an attitude of mind we shall never experience any sorrow whatsoever but shall attain transcendent peace.

★

Gopīs' Unalloyed Love or Secret of Rāsa-Līlā

In the following lines we venture to put on record some thoughts on what goes by the name of "Rāsa-Pañcādhyāyī" (Discourses 29 to 33 of Book X of *Śrīmad Bhāgavata),* which relate to the famous Rāsa Dance of Bhagavān Śrī Kṛṣṇa. The true meaning of this *Rāsa-Pañcādhyāyī* is quite different from the interpretation which is generally put on it. In reality, the *Rāsa-Pañcādhyāyī* depicts the unalloyed love of the Gopīs (the cowherdesses of Vraja) for Bhagavān Śrī Kṛṣṇa. It is due to the aforesaid unadulterated love that such a universal tribute of praise is paid to the Gopīs today. Among the Gopīs again Śrī Rādhā occupies the highest place; She is the Hlādinī Śakti (Delighting Potency) of the Lord. It was given to Śrī Rādhā alone to gladden Śrī Kṛṣṇa the Ruler of the countless millions of universes—to afford Him delight and joy. Her female companions, the Gopīs, too shared this role of Śrī Rādhā. Of all the books depicting the pastimes of Lord Śrī Kṛṣṇa, we recognize *Śrīmad Bhāgavata* as the foremost. But our mind refuses to swallow the few stray references in the *Bhāgavata,* smacking of liaison. They are of no use to us; it should be our concern to read therein unalloyed love alone. Conjugal love can be sexual; but we can never believe even in a dream that the Lord's love for the Gopīs was of a sexual type. The love of Bhagavān Śrī Kṛṣṇa for Śrī Rukmiṇī (His premier Spouse), through whom He begot children, had a divine touch about it. Sexual love is no love. The Lord is Love and Bliss personified. The love of Bhagavān Śrī Kṛṣṇa was absolutely unalloyed. All His gestures during the Rāsa Dance had the sole motive of gladdening the Gopīs. Whatever He did in course of His Rāsa-Līlā viz., His dancing, His singing, His playing on the Flute and everything else was intended only to delight the Gopīs, to enhance their love. Similarly every gesture of the Gopīs was actuated by the sole desire of gladdening Him.

Lord Śrī Kṛṣṇa was none else than the Supreme Spirit, the

Supreme Brahma; the sole purpose of His descent in a human semblance was to propagate love and not to indulge in self-gratification. And, as a matter of fact, it was unalloyed love that He actually did propagate. I remember to have heard a popular legend, which runs as follows. Once upon a time the sage Nārada chanced to meet the god of love, and said, "Hullo, Love, you were able to kindle the flame of passion in me too !" To this Love gave a most presumptuous reply. He said, "I hold you in no account; I can infatuate and make a puppet of even Brahmā, Viṣṇu and Maheśa. None can stand before me." Thereupon Nārada called on Lord Viṣṇu and repeated to Him verbatim the braggadocio of Love. "The fellow has become so arrogant," he added, "that he considers You as of little consequence; if You take no steps to curb his pride, he will grow all the more impertinent. Hence You should root out his vanity." Lord Viṣṇu asked Nārada to tell Love that He would assume a human personality in the following Dvāpara age, and expected Love to let Him know whether He should meet him in open combat or whether He should give battle from behind a fortification. When Nārada delivered the Lord's message to Love, he arrogantly said, "None can worst me even from behind a fortification, much less in open combat."*

When Nārada communicated Love's reply to the Lord, the latter sent word to him through Nārada that He would assume the form of Śrī Kṛṣṇa only to encounter him in open combat. It was now the time for Him to redeem His word of honour. To say nothing of the Lord, what actually happened was that even the Gopīs who participated in His Rāsa Dance trampled the

* Giving battle from behind a fortification means living in a secluded place such as a mountain cave or an unfrequented forest—where there is hardly any occasion for the flame of passion being aroused—and curbing the sexual urge by observing a vow of strict celibacy; while meeting Love in open combat means conquering the sexual urge even though living in the company of women as a householder.

pride of Love. In the captivating woodland of Vṛndāvana where a cool, soft and fragrant breeze blew—which naturally tended to kindle the flame of passion, and which we calculated to infatuate with love even sages and hermits—those charming cowherd damsels and young matrons exhibited such a thorough mastery of the self that the darts of Love proved altogether ineffectual against them. That host of pretty girls conquered Love and danced on his head, crushing his pride. Even though they blended in their person comeliness with blooming youth, their behaviour throughout the Rāsa Dance was marked by pure love and nothing but love. In this way when the Gopīs themselves were able to conquer Love, it was something much easier for the Lord, who is ever free from all bondage.

In the Rāsa-Līlā we find a display of art in the form of dancing, singing and playing on the Flute, prompted by pure love. There is no tinge of sexuality in it. Lord Śrī Kṛṣṇa fanned the flame of unadulterated love in the heart of the Gopīs. He danced in their company in the course of the Rāsa-Līlā thereby bringing them supreme delight and creating an atmosphere of unalloyed love. In that ecstasy of joy they remembered nothing but themselves and their divine Lover. The god of love could not even gaze on them. We shall presently see how pure their love was. The Lord poured forth a most ravishing melody on His flute in order to attract the Gopīs to that beautiful spot. The moment the Gopīs heard the strain they ran up to the Lord, abandoning all their duties. On that occasion the Lord addressed the Gopīs in the following words:—"O blessed ones, nights are generally very frightful and this woodland is infested by ferocious animals. Therefore, do you return all of you to Vraja without further delay. Women should not stay in a dreadful forest like this overnight. Your parents, husband and children and other relations too must be missing you and looking out for you. Do not make them feel apprehensive on your account. You have now witnessed the charms of this forest, laden as it is with flowers of diverse hues. Lo ! It has been illumined by the soft rays of the moon as though the moon-god has painted it in glowing colours with his own hands. And the tender shoots of trees gently waving in the cool breeze coming from the Yamunā side are enhancing the beauties of this forest. But now that you have seen all this you had better return to Vraja as soon as possible and should not tarry here any longer. You all come of respectable families and possess a noble character. Therefore, go and wait upon your husbands. If you have been drawn to this place by ties of affection for Me, you are guilty of no unseemly behaviour; it is quite in the fitness of things that you should have done so. For even birds and beasts love Me and feel delighted to see Me. But the paramount duty of a married woman, O blessed ladies, is to minister to her husband and his kinsmen in a guileless spirit and to nourish her children. O Gopīs fondness for Me is not developed so much by physical proximity to Me as by hearing of My pastimes and virtues, by the sight of My form, by contemplating on Me and by singing of My glories. Therefore, return to your homes at once."

The Gopīs replied, "Beloved Śrī Kṛṣṇa, being the indweller of all hearts, You know the inmost secrets of our heart. It does not befit You to speak in this cruel strain. Abandoning everything else, we have bestowed our heart on Your feet alone. Dear Śrī Kṛṣṇa, You know the essence of all Dharmas. You are quite right when You say that it is the natural duty of a married woman to serve her husband and sons and other relations. But it is You alone whom we should wait upon even if we abide by Your instructions; for You are none else than God, the object aimed at by all teachings. You are disinterested friend, nay, the very Self, the darling of all living beings."

Thereafter the Lord most fondly commenced His Rāsa Dance in the company of all those Gopīs. Bhagavān Śrī Kṛṣṇa, who is the Master of all Yogas, assumed as many forms as the Gopīs and placed Himself between every two Gopīs. In this way He started dancing with them in a ring, one form of the Lord appearing by the side of each Gopī. Every single Gopī felt the presence of her beloved Śrī Kṛṣṇa solely by her side. In that blessed hour all the divinities appeared on the scene alongwith their spouses to witness the Rāsa festival. Drums in heaven sounded of their own accord. Heavenly flowers rained. Gandharvas (celestial musicians) sang the bright glories of the Lord alongwith their wives. As the Gopīs danced with their most beloved Śyāmasundara their wristlets and anklets as well as the tiny bells of their girdle jingled altogether, producing a loud chime. Dancing on the beautiful sands of the Yamunā in the midst of that company of charming women Lord Śrī Kṛṣṇa presented a unique sight. He shone like an emerald of most exquisite beauty threaded with a multitude of gold beads. In the course of that unearthly dance the Gopīs set down their feet in a variety of artistic ways. Now they placed their foot ahead and now in the rear. Now they trod with slow paces and now with great rapidity and at times they whirled like a top. Now they gesticulated with uplifted hands and now they smiled and at other times they made amorous gestures with their eye-brows. Their earrings swung against their cheeks. Drops of perspiration appeared on their faces due to the exertion caused by dancing. In this way the Gopīs sang and danced in the company of their beloved Lord. At that time the numerous swarthy forms of Śrī Kṛṣṇa appeared like so many clouds, while the fair-complexioned Gopīs moving in their midst shone like flashes of lightning.

When the Lord, who is omnipresent and the crest-jewel of all generous-minded souls, honoured the Gopīs as aforesaid, they thought they were superior to every other woman in the whole universe—that there was none who could equal them. Seeing that pride had sprouted in the heart of the Gopīs, the Lord disappeared from their midst alongwith His chief companion. Śrī Rādhā, just in order to humble their pride. The dramatic disappearance of the Lord from the scene caused a flutter in the ranks of the Gopīs. They felt extremely distressed at the separation from their beloved Lord and started their quest for Him in the forest. When the Lord could not be found even after a diligent search, they began to imitate the pastimes of the Lord in their own midst. Some personated Śrī Kṛṣṇa, while others played the Gopīs. In this way they repeated the Rāsa Dance.

Anant Śrī Kṛṣṇa, as the Lord was rambling in the forest in the company of Śrī Rādhā, the latter too felt proud to think the Lord had chosen to take Her alongwith Him to the exclusion of others, which clearly demonstrated that She was superior to all the other Gopīs. Now in the course of their wanderings Śrī Rādhā told the Lord that She was too tired to walk any more, and accordingly requested Him to carry Her on His shoulders. The Lord readily acquiesced and sank low as if ready to lift Her on His shoulders. But the moment Śrī Rādhā strode across His shoulder the Lord vanished. Śrī Rādhā too wailed and wept at the sudden disappearance of the Lord and proceeded in quest of the Lord, rending the air with the cries of "Kṛṣṇa, O Kṛṣṇa !" She too now realized that the Lord had forsaken Her only because She had felt proud of Her superior luck. She resumed Her search with renewed vigour.

On the other side the Gopīs too roamed about in the forest in search of Lord Śrī Kṛṣṇa and Śrī Rādhā. In the course of their quest they came across the footprints of both. Following those footprints, the Gopīs proceeded onward. Going further they discovered the traces of Śrī Kṛṣṇa having sat down; but still further they found the footprints of Śrī Rādhā alone and not of Śrī Kṛṣṇa. The Gopīs advanced with the footprints of Śrī Rādhā and at some distance they found Śrī Rādhā crying in distress. The Gopīs enquired the whereabouts of Śrī Kṛṣṇa from Śrī Rādhā, who told them how the Lord had accompanied Her to that spot and then left Her too. She further told them that the Lord had forsaken them only because they felt proud of their good luck, just in order to cure them of their pride, and that they should all pray to Him imploring Him to appear again.

Now the Gopīs who were all distressed on account of their separation from the Lord, cried out to the Lord in deep anguish. Finding them sore at heart, the Lord appeared in their midst once more as suddenly as He had vanished.

The Gopīs now addressed the following questions to the Lord.

"Kṛṣṇa !" they said, "there are some people who only requite the love they receive from others, while others love even those who do not love them; and there are still others who love not even those who love them, much less those that do not love them. Pray, tell us which of these types You like best."

"My beloved Gopīs !" Replied the Lord, "those who merely reciprocate the love they receive from others are selfish people. Their behaviour is characterized neither by friendliness nor by virtue. Their love is actuated by self-interest; it has no other motive. The heart of those, on the other hand, who love even such people as do not return their love—e.g., loving parents and men who are compassionate by nature—is full of goodwill and benevolence and their behaviour is marked by artless virtue too. There is a fourth type of men who do not love even those who love them, much less those who do not love them. These people fall under four categories. (1) they who revel in their own Self; (2) they who have gained their desire, i.e., who have realized their object in life; (3) ungrateful souls and (4) they who deliberately seek to harm even their well-wishers and benefactors in the shape of their elders. As for myself, dear friends, I do not reciprocate the love of those who love Me, even as I should Just as a pauper who stumbles on a fortune and then loses it, is ever filled with the thought of that lost treasure, and thinks of nothing else, even so I behave like that only in order that the thought of My lovers may be concentrated on Me all the more and incessantly too. I screened Myself from your view only in order to cure you of your pride and enhance your love, so that your thought might be reveted on Me and might not wander. Please, therefore, do not find fault with My love. You are all dear to Me as I am to you. Your meeting with Me here is altogether free from blemish and beyond reproach. I cannot repay the debt I owe to you even if I serve you in return with an immortal body for countless years. I shall remain ever indebted to you." Saying so the Lord commenced His Rāsa Dance with the Gopīs once more.

The Gopīs had no tinge of carnality in them. As for Lord Śrī Kṛṣṇa, He was above sexuality; nay, by His contact the sensual craving in the Gopīs too had altogether vanished. Lord Śrī Kṛṣṇa later on had as many as sixteen thousand, one hundred and eight wedded wives and through them He begot more than a lakh of sons. Nevertheless He had no tinge of carnality in Him. He simply behaved with the ladies as one would with his wives in conformity with the injunctions of the Śastras and that too without any sensuality.

Even then if anyone imagines that the Lord had illicit connection with the Gopīs I can only say that the fellow will get no room even in hell. Concupiscence dare not enter the mind of the Lord or the Gopīs; on the other hand, their very thought can purge one's mind of lust. The very talk of the Gopīs drives away sensuality. I cannot imagine what destiny awaits those who hold that the Gopīs were guilty of adultery. The Lord Himself spoke very highly of the Gopīs. The Gopīs belonged to the weaker sex in the first instance and women are said to be eight times more passionate than men. Then there was the Supreme Deity Himself by their side in the form of Śrī Kṛṣṇa, whose comeliness of person was nonpareil. All that is beautiful in this creation cannot equal, even when taken together a fraction of the Lord's trasncendent beauty. The Gopīs remained wholly above carnality even in the presence of the supremely beautiful; hence they cannot be overpraised. The Gopīs possessed such marvellous power that he who beheld them was rid of all sensual craving; how, then, could they arouse passion in the heart of the Lord, whose very thought dispels all concupiscence ? Appearing in the most attractive form of Śrī Kṛṣṇa, that Supreme Deity curbed the pride of Love and taught to the world the lesson of passionlessness in all circumstances. Every single conduct of the Lord was exemplary. He testifies to this in His own words in the *Gītā*—

न मे पार्थास्ति कर्तव्यं त्रिषु लोकेषु किंचन।
नानवाप्तमवाप्तव्यं वर्त एव च कर्मणि॥
यदि ह्यहं न वर्तेयं जातु कर्मण्यतन्द्रितः।
मम वर्त्मानुवर्तन्ते मनुष्याः पार्थ सर्वशः॥
उत्सीदेयुरिमे लोका न कुर्यां कर्म चेदहम्।
संकरस्य च कर्ता स्यामुपहन्यामिमाः प्रजाः॥ (III.22—24)

"Arjuna, there is nothing in all the three worlds for Me to do, nor is there anything worth attaining unattained by Me; yet I persist in My activity. If I do not engage in action scrupulously at any time, great harm will come to the world; for, Arjuna, men follow My way in all matters. If I cease to act, these worlds will perish; nay, I should prove to be the cause of confusion, as well as of the destruction of these people."

Let us ponder over the fact that if the Lord were guilty of adultery with the Gopīs, He should have earned the epithet of an adulterer. On the other hand, when Uttarā, the widow of Abhimanyu, delivered Parīkṣit as a still-born child, the Lord expressed His wish in the following memorable words that the child might come back to life. "If I have adhered to My vow of truthfulness throughout My life," He said, "if I have practised continence from the very beginning of My life till this day, let this blessed child of Uttarā come back to life !" Life returned to the child the moment He uttered these words. From this incident it can be easily understood that the miracle could not have happened had the Lord been the least guilty of moral turpitude. Again, Śiśupāla was a sworn enemy of Śrī Kṛṣṇa. We are told at length in the *Sabhā-Parva* of the *Mahābhārata* how he poured a volley of abuses on the Lord in open assembly. We are further told in the *Gadā-Parva* of the same great epic how Duryodhana too rained abuses on Him while dying. Had the Lord been the least guilty of illicit intercourse Śiśupāla and Duryodhana would have surely referred to His connection with the Gopīs while abusing Him. But they did not utter a word about it. This testifies to the fact that Śrī Kṛṣṇa's moral character was reputed to be above suspicion even in those days. That is the reason why Śiśupāla and Duryodhana failed to cast any aspersion against His character. They would not have spared Him if they had the least suspicion about His character. Besides this, Śrī Kṛṣṇa was only ten years of age at the time of the Rāsa-Dānce. By no stretch of imagination can a boy of ten years be suspected of sexual intercourse. Hence it cannot be imagined that Śrī Kṛṣṇa had the least tinge of immorality in Him. Only dissemblers and those given to adultery level such false accusations against the Lord and, in order to gratify their base passions, impudently declare that the Lord had sexual commerce with the Gopīs, and that it was their intercourse with the Lord which brought emancipation to them. Through such mischievous statements they inveigle innocent and guileless women and, themselves posing as Śrī Kṛṣṇa, treat those unfortunate women as Gopīs and then make them victims of their lust. The Lord Himself knows what terrible retribution lies in store for such wretched and perverse souls.

Bhagavān Śrī Kṛṣṇa's relation with the Gopīs was marked by pure love; there was no trace of sensuality in it. The love He bore to them had nothing in common with that of a paramour for his beloved. I dare not say that the treatment of love in the *Bhāgavata* is sparse in comparison to other works. The subject has been dealt with at length in *Śrīmad Bhāgavata.* Only the love that has been discussed therein is absolutely unalloyed and stainless; there is no tinge of carnality in it. Certainly there are some obscene references in a few verses of *Śrīmad Bhāgavata* and the love of a paramour also finds mention therein. We shall not be within our rights if we reject these verses as interpolated nor shall we be justified in straining these passages and putting a Vedantic interpretation on them. We should not, however, construe the obscene expressions used in such verses in their literal and etymological sense; for Bhagavān Śrī Kṛṣṇa was absolutely free from all blemish. being no other than the supreme Brahma, who is Truth, Consciousness and Bliss solidified and wholly untainted by Māyā. Hence we are not prepared to believe that Śrī Kṛṣṇa could ever transgress the bounds of propriety nor do we gain anything by such belief; for such a belief is neither warranted by the scriptures nor corroborated by reason. There is no deviation from the established doctrine. The love of Śrī Kṛṣṇa for the Gopīs was altogether unalloyed; it had no carnal touch about it. Nevertheless the lewd expressions found here and there about Śrī Kṛṣṇa bringing under suspicion His relation with the Gopīs, baffle our understanding and should not, therefore, be taken as correct. Instead of calling in question the authority or authenticity of *Śrīmad Bhāgavata* we should only concede that we fail to grasp the true meaning of such references. In this way a believing man should confess the bluntness of his intellect rather than cast a slur on the Lord, *Śrīmad Bhāgavata* or the Gopīs.

Similarly if anyone accuses exalted personages like Śrī Balarāma of drunkenness, adultery and so on, how can we reconcile ourselves to such a view ? Wherever there are references to lying, deceit, thieving, adultery, drinking and other vices that have been universally condemned, they can never apply to the Lord and His devotees. One cannot imagine that such vices exist in them. If a man like me should resort to thieving, dishonesty, adultery and so on, can you ever believe that anything and everything I do is right, and that I am above all criticism ? No, such a conduct on my part can never be pardonable. If I defend myself, I shall be deceiving the world, and will be guilty of an abominable act. Anyone who claims to be an exalted soul, a man possessing supernatural powers, and preaches that God and holy men can never do wrong—'whatever they do is right—and thereby invites members of the opposite sex to have carnal enjoyment with him, take it from me, such a man can never be a saint. Nay, he is a great hypocrite, an adulterer, an aspirant to honour and fame and a great impostor. A man should never allow himself to be misled by such rogues and dissemblers. The pastimes of Lord Śrī Kṛṣṇa as well as the *Rāsa-Pañcādhyāyī* of *Śrīmad Bhāgavata* are absolutely above suspicion. Nay, anyone who is sincerely devoted to this *Rāsa-Pañcādhyāyī* speedily develops love for the Lord and even the last traces of sensuality that may be lurking in his heart are obliterated by the grace of the Lord.

In the last issue of the "Kalyana-Kalpataru" I discussed some points relating to the Rāsa-Līlā. Barring a few verses, which contain some undisguised erotic references and obscene expressions, everything else in the *Rāsa-Pañcādhyāyī* is such as goes to intensify pure love. It deserves to be reverently studied and the reader will be well-advised to keep his eye fixed on unalloyed love and maintain a pure outlook. If our heart is dominated by pure and genuine love, we shall find our voice chocked with emotion, the hair on our body will stand on their end and our limbs will begin to quiver. Excess of love chockes one's throat and voice and brings tears to one's eyes. The eye-lids forget to fall when the charming figure of the beloved Śyāmasundara appears before one's eyes; for the eyes begin to drink His beauty. Everything is possible in the sphere of love. If there is pure and highly developed reverence and love, one can experience these things. Lord Śrī Kṛṣṇa is an unfathomable ocean of bliss; the Gopīs danced to His tune. They carried out all His behests, were ever at His beck and call.

One may ask here: if the Gopīs were at His beck and call, how is it that they did not return to their home in obedience to His command when the Lord asked them to do so ? Our reply to this is that the Gopīs found themselves so overpowered with love that their feet refused to move. Their legs were paralyzed as it were. We have the Gopīs' own testimony on this point. They said:—

चित्तं सुखेन भवतापहृतं गृहेषु
यन्निर्विशत्युत करावपि गृह्यकृत्ये ।
पादौ पदं न चलतस्तव पादमूलाद्
यामः कथं व्रजमथो करवाम किं वा ॥

(*Śrīmad Bhāgavata* X.xxix.34)

"You have easily stolen our heart, which was attached to our home, and robbed us of our hands too, which were employed in our household duties; while our feet refuse to move even a step

away from the soles of Your feet. How, then, shall we return to Vraja or what shall we do (even if we go there) ?"

In the *Padma-Purāṇa* we read how on hearing of the malicious gossip against Śrī Sītā, Śrī Rāma commanded His younger brothers, Bharata and Śatrughna, to leave Her in the woods near the hermitage of the sage Vālmīki. Bharata and Śatrughna, however, were taken aback to hear this command and fainted. They did not deliberately flout His order; yet they found themselves unable to carry it out. The same thing applies to the case of the Gopīs too.

Truly speaking, Śrī Bhagavān is the supreme Lord of all; hence the Gopīs were perfectly justified in going to Him. The commands of Śrī Bhagavān carry even greater weight than the injunctions of the Smṛti-texts; for He is the supreme Lord. Even the order of a husband is secondary as compared to His command. The Gopīs were so overwhelmed with love for the Lord that they would not heed any remonstrance. When they heard the call of the Lord's Flute, they could not resist it. In the helplessness brought about by excess of love they abandoned all their household work as it was and ran up to Him.

The story how Lord Viṣṇu told Nārada that He would descend in the form of Śrī Kṛṣṇa in the Dvāpara age in order to humble the pride of Love has been handed down to us by tradition. The readers of this book too might have heard such a story. My heart gives credit to it and it is just possible that the story may be found in some scripture too. It is an open secret that many of our sacred books were destroyed during the Muslim rule. Hence this story should be believed as true even if we fail to come across it in any of our scriptures; for it inculcates a truth which is at once transcendental, profound, logical and glorifying pure love.

The Gopīs' love for Lord Śrī Kṛṣṇa was of the purest type and transcendental in character; there was no tinge of lewdness or sensuality in it. The Lord felt enchanted by their overpowering love and the Gopīs too forgot their very self under the all-conquering influence of the Lord's Love. The Lord melted as it were at the very sight of the Gopīs and *vice versa,* even as the gem known by the name of Candrakānta is supposed to exude nectar when moonbeams fall on it. Although we have only heard of such a gem and never beheld it with our own eyes, references to it may be found in our sacred books. If an insentient object like the Candrakānta gem can exude nectar under the influence of the moon, it is no wonder that devotees should melt at the sight of the Lord. The Lord may be compared to the moon, His love to the moonbeams and His devotees may be likened to the Candrakānta gem. We read in the scriptures how even stones melted under the softening influence of the Lord's love. It is much easier to conceive, then, that His devotees should so melt.

The Lord, His love and His lovers are identical in substance. They are all spiritual and divine in essence, transcendental in character. That is why those who love Him from the bottom of their heart are translated to His transcendental and divine Abode. The Lord is Truth, Consciousness and Bliss personified and His lover too acquires the same character while leaving his mortal coil and departing to His divine Abode.

The Gopīs have been classified in our scriptures into several groups. Some of them have been declared to be the incarnations of Śrutis (Vedic texts), while others had been sages and hermits in their previous existence. A third group is stated to have descended from the Lord's own divine Abode alongwith the Lord and in the manner of the Lord in order to participate in His Līlā and fulfil His mission of propagating true love. From this we can form an idea as to how wonderful and exalted the Gopīs were. When the Lord asked them to return to Vraja, they made the following reply. "You are no mere delighter of Yaśodā; You are the transcendental Brahma, the supreme Spirit, the suzerain Lord of the whole universe. It is, therefore, our paramount duty to seek Your presence and wait upon You, our supreme Master.

Such was the ideal love of the Gopīs ! It would be the height of folly on one's part to scent carnality in the behaviour of the

Gopīs, whose very thought eradicates sexuality. On the other hand, one should believe and feel sure that their very sight could obliterate all traces of sensuality in one's mind. The Gopīs cherished a most sublime type of love for the Lord. The wives of the Brāhmaṇa priests of Mathurā too were similar devotees of the Lord. Once they took salvers full of delicacies for the Lord, who happened to be in their vicinity. But they too were prompted by no erotic sentiment; they sought His presence with the purest of motives. Their people too put no ban on their meeting with the Lord. Even if they tried to restrain them, they would not have voluntarily submitted to such restraint; and had they been detained by force, their soul would have thrown off all barriers and met the Lord before all the rest. The affection of the sages' wives was unsullied; they loved Him as the Supreme Deity.

As for Śrī Rādhā's love it is needless to say that it was absolutely unalloyed. She had no shadow of carnality in Her. She was no other than the loving potency of the Lord and had descended for the sole purpose of contributing to His joy. Their conviviality and hilarious enjoyment and exchange of love were only a part of Their divine sport. Both were identical. Both ever continued to delight each other.

Of all the types of mental attitude cultivated in relation to the Lord, such as Vātsalya (parental affection), Kāntabhāva (conjugal love), Dāsya (the attitude of the servitor) and Śāntabhāva (the attitude of complete resignation to the Lord), the sentiment of pure love or Mādhurya as it is called is the best and worthy of the highest esteem. It transcends all other sentiments. It is higher even than the feeling of Devotion; it is the very fruit of Devotion. In this sentiment there is complete identity between the lover and the Beloved, an identity which has no parallel anywhere. The two hands become as good as one when their palms are joined together. The type of identity existing between the lover and the Beloved here may be compared to the oneness of the joined hands. But even this illustration is not quite apt; for the lover and the Beloved here are ever united in a a peculiar bond. The river Gaṅgā falls into the ocean and becomes one with it. Then it is known by the name of ocean alone; it no longer retains its separate name or form. At Prayag the streams of the Gaṅgā and the Yamunā unite with each other; but thereafter the united stream bears the name of Gaṅgā alone, the Yamunā no longer retains its separate name or form. Just as all the rivers falling into the ocean lose their identity, it is the ocean alone that remains, even so the devotees who get merged in the Lord, become one with Him and no longer retain their separate name or form, it is the Lord alone who remains. But the identity between the lover and the Beloved in this plane is not of the type mentioned in the above illustrations. Here the two, though identical in substance, retain separate forms for the sake of the Līlā (Sport).

Lord Śrī Kṛṣṇa and Śrī Rādhā both are love personified. Every gesture of Śrī Kṛṣṇa is intended to delight Śrī Rādhā and every movement of Śrī Rādhā is likewise intended to enrapture Śrī Kṛṣṇa. The love that inspires Them is ineffable, it cannot be described in words. It was to reveal this love that Lord Śrī Kṛṣṇa manifested Himself on earth.

When such a love as inspired Śrī Kṛṣṇa and Śrī Rādhā is developed, all disparity between the lover and the Beloved disappears. Where there is the attitude of a servitor the Lord is the master and the devotee, His servant. But no such distinction exists in the realm of supreme love mentioned above; here the lover and the Beloved are absolutely one. Transcending every other attitude the lover in this plane becomes one with the Beloved. In order to illustrate the attitude of a servitor let us take the example of Hanumān. Hanumān would never have the audacity to share the seat of his Master, Śrī Rāma, even when invited by the Lord. He would meekly decline the offer, saying that such a behaviour on his part would amount to a flagrant breach of propriety. It would be altogether unbecoming on the part of a servant to occupy the seat of his master. Of course, Hanumān was ever prepared to render all forms of service to the Lord. In the domain of love adumbrated above there is no such distinction. It is a state of self-forgetfulness. Here both take delight in gladdening each other. To take the illustration of the two hands, both are equal in our eyes. For the sake of purity we observe a distinction between the two, recognizing the right hand as superior and the left as inferior. From the point of view of the self, however, the right hand is as much ourselves as the left. If an abscess is formed in our left hand, we shall try to get rid of it as quickly as we shall do in the case of the right. We shall never neglect it because it is inferior.

Similarly a devoted wife takes every care to avoid anything which may prove unpalatable to her lord. She is ever obedient to him and her behaviour towards him is full of consideration, esteem and regard. When, however, one reaches the stage of supreme love, which—as we have pointed out above—transcends all other attitudes of mind, the spirit of obedience is no longer there nor has one any regard, consideration or respect for the other; for there is absolute equality between the lover and the Beloved in that realm. This stage of love transcends the three Guṇas or modes of Prakṛti. The love which has reached this stage does not take its stand on noble qualities and glory, it is spontaneous in character; for it is a purely spiritual state standing above all virtue and glory.

The above-mentioned attitude of love is superior even to the attitude of Vātsalya (parental affection). Mother Yaśodā, for instance, who is the model of parental affection, intimidates the Lord by showing to Him a cudgel and the Lord too crouches with fear at the sight of the cudgel. In the attitude of love, however, which is absolutely fearless, there is no such intimidation or fear even in external behaviour. Where the two become one, who should fear whom ?

Even in the attitude of friendship (Sakhya-bhāva) we sometimes observe a mixture of fear and reverence. When the Lord revealed His cosmic form before His intimate friend Arjuna, the latter trembled to see that wonderful figure and began to extol the Lord and addressed a prayer to Him. The Lord then consoled His beloved friend in the following words:—

मा ते व्यथा मा च विमूढभावो
दृष्ट्वा रूपं घोरमीदृङ्ममेदम्।
व्यपेतभीः प्रीतमनाः पुनस्त्वं
तदेव मे रूपमिदं प्रपश्य ॥

"Seeing such a frightful form of Mine as this, be not perturbed or perplexed; with a fearless and complacent mind behold once again the same four-armed form of Mine."

In this way the Lord assured His frightened friend that they were always one and that he had no reason to get afraid of Him.

He, however, who has risen above the attitude of a friend and has reached the stage of supreme love no longer retains any shadow of reverence, regard, esteem, fear, shyness and so on. The lover and the Beloved both become love incarnate as it were in that stage. It is sheer folly to conceive any disparity between the two. In reality the devotee and the Lord are one undivided mass of love, appearing divided only in outward form.

One can be redeemed by the mere sight and touch of a devotee who has reached this stage or by mere conversation with him. Only one must have reverence for him. Of all such lovers as have attained to this stage, Śrī Rādhā occupies the highest place. She is unrivalled in Her love for Śrī Kṛṣṇa, Śrī Rukmiṇī embodies the divine glory of the Lord. When the great devotee Sudāmā called on Śrī Kṛṣṇa in His palace at Dvārakā, the Lord was overwhelmed with emotion to see His erstwhile chum in that wretched condition. Sudāmā had brought with him a small bundle of parched rice as a present for the Lord from his wife; but he was taken aback at the sight of the royal splendour in the midst of which Śrī Kṛṣṇa was living. The Lord at once perceived the demur the destitute Brāhmaṇa naturally felt in handing over his poor present and snatched the bundle concealed in his arm-pit. The tattered piece of cloth in the end of which the parched rice were tied gave way when pulled by the Lord and the grains of rice were strewn all over the bejewelled floor. The Lord fell on the scattered grains like a famished man and, picking them with His own hands, began to eat them with great relish. When He had taken two handfuls in His mouth and was about to take a third, Śrī Rukmiṇī, who was His divine glory personified, intervened and wrested the present from Her lord. "Are You going to bestow Your entire fortune on the Brāhmaṇa ?" She protested. In this way Rukmiṇī was reminded of Her affluence. Had Śrī Rādhā been in Her place, She would never have deterred the Lord from giving away His fortune. She could immolate Her own self for the sake of the Lord. Śrī Rukmiṇī too was in no way deficient; but it must be conceded that Śrī Rādhā outmatched Her. The fortune of all the three worlds put together is of no value in the eyes of him who has transcended the three Gunas. Śrī Kṛṣṇa and Śrī Rādhā both are beyond the realm of the three Guṇas. Śrī Rādhā can, therefore, never be swayed by the three Guṇas. Pure love is just the same as Brahma, who is Truth, Consciousness and Bliss solidified. As for the joy that seems to flow from the divine splendour, it is only a reflection of the all-blissful Lord, and not His essence.

Some people hold a different opinion on the subject. They say it is love that manifests itself in two forms—Energy (Śakti) and the Energizer (Śaktimān). Śrī Rādhā is the Energy and Śrī Kṛṣṇa, the Energizer. But the supreme love discussed in the foregoing paragraphs is higher even than this love. In this state, which transcends all other attitudes of mind, there is identity between the two. The Energy and the Energizer are no longer divided here; the two are reduced to one. The duality is only apparent. Rādhā and Kṛṣṇa are really one. The Gopīs' love for Śrī Kṛṣṇa was similar in character. If anyone smells sensuality in this love, it reflects on his own character. There is no shadow of bashfulness, diffidence, fear or carnality in it.

Besides this, contact with the Lord in any form leads to final beatitude. Thought of the Lord inspired by ill-will or fear as in the case of Mārīca (the maternal uncle of Rāvaṇa) and Kaṁsa (Śrī Kṛṣṇa's own maternal uncle) can bring redemption to one's soul. If anyone seeks liberation through liaison with the Lord we have no objection to his or her doing so. But such an attitude towards the Lord is not at all worthy of esteem. Surely the Gopīs' had no such relation with the Lord; their love for the Lord was of the highest and purest form. Although it is doubtless true that even Pūtanā, who gave a poisonous suck to the Lord, attained liberation thereby, the conduct of Pūtanā was in no way worth imitating. Even so Rāvaṇa met the Lord in a hostile encounter and secured liberation; but even his behaviour towards the Lord was anything but ideal. Therefore, even if we were to get liberation through liaison or hatred, such a liberation would be worth rejecting. For it would be sheer folly on our part to cultivate an attitude of illicit intimacy or hatred towards the Lord in preference to the attitude of a servitor, friendship, parental affection, complete resignation or pure love cultivated in a spirit of reverence, affection and devotion. One should maintain a relation of pure love with the Lord; this alone can bring us redemption at the earliest moment.

The Gopīs' attitude towards the Lord was one of pure love, which elicited a tribute of unqualified praise from Uddhava. Had it not been so, Uddhava could not have spoken so highly of them. It was their unalloyed love which astonished and amazed Uddhava.

Hence we should try our best to cultivate unalloyed love for the Lord in aforesaid manner.

Exclusive and Unalloyed Love for God: The Benevolence of God

Love for God is ineffable in character. Even those who love Him cannot describe it; what, then, shall I say about it ? In fact, human speech is incapable of depicting the true character of love, which is a feeling embedded in the deepest recesses of the heart. Certain outward signs manifest themselves in the person of a man in whose heart love is awakened. Such symptoms too appear only in the stage of Sādhanā (striving). When the emotion of love is aroused in the heart, sometimes the hair on the body stands erect, while at other times tears gush out of one's eyes, the throat gets choked and speech begins to falter. These are the outward manifestations of Love. Even as the emotion grows more intense, the lover gets inwardly enraptured and in that ecstasy of love he forgets his own self. For example, when a cake is fried in boiling ghee, it rolls about and remains unsteady so long as it is raw; and it becomes still and inactive when it gets thoroughly cooked. Similarly during the stage of Sādhanā love for God often comes to the surface and manifests itself through signs of the type mentioned above. When, however, the heart is full of love, a man becomes mute like a dumb fellow and gets immersed in love. And when a man gets immersed in love, God-Realization comes to him. But he himself is unable to describe the transcendental state which he experiences when he has actually realized God. For in that state he forgets his own self and God-consciousness alone remains. When he looks at the lotus-like countenance of the Lord, his gaze gets fixed on it in the same way as the eyes of the Cakora bird get reveted on the orb of the moon on a full-moon day. He gets so enraptured at the sight of the Lord's personality that he forgets everything other than the Lord.

Gosvāmī Tulasīdāsa finds himself utterly incapable of describing the transcendent outburst of emotion that Bharata felt when he met Śrī Rāma at Citrakūṭa. He says—

*"How can the love that characterized the meeting (of Bharata and Śrī Rāma) be described ? It was beyond conception, expression or emulation to the race of bards. The two brothers were full of supreme affection; their mind and reason, intellect and individuality were all lost. Tell me, who can give utterance to such a noble love ? Whose shadow will the poet's mind be guided by ? The poet's solid strength lies in the theme to be worked upon and the expression he would use. A dancer regulates his movements according to the cadence of the accompanying music. Unapproachable was the affection of Bharata and the Chief of Raghu's line, which is beyond the conception of Brahmā (the creator), Śrī Hari (Lord Viṣṇu) and Hara (Lord Śiva). How, then, can I describe it, dull-witted as I am ? Can an instrument strung with a chord made of Gander (a species of grass) produce good music ?"**

When the Lord returned to Ayodhyā from Laṅkā and saw Bharata and Śatrughna, the scene of love that followed their meeting was altogether indescribable. Although we did not find it mentioned in any book, we have heard it said that Vibhīṣaṇa and Sugrīva, who were present on the occasion, burst into tears when they witnessed the unique love of the four brothers and contrasted it with their own attitude towards their brothers,

* मिलनि प्रीति किमि जाइ बखानी। कबिकुल अगम करम मन बानी॥
परम प्रेम पूरन दोउ भाई। मन बुधि चित अहमिति बिसराई॥
कहहु सुपेम प्रगट को करई। केहि छाया कबि मति अनुसरई॥
कबिहि अरथ आखर बलु साँचा। अनुहरि ताल गतिहि नटु नाचा॥
अगम सनेह भरत रघुबर को। जहँ न जाइ मनु बिधि हरि हर को॥
सो मैं कुमति कहौं केहि भाँती। बाज सुराग कि गाँडर ताँती॥

Rāvaṇa and Vālī, whose destruction they had sought and actually brought about at the hands of the Lord. The thought filled them with shame and remorse; but alas ! The error could no longer be rectified.

Among the characters figuring in the *Rāmacaritamānasa* of Gosvāmī Tulasīdāsa, the love of Sutīkṣṇa too is most wonderful. The play of emotions in his heart at the time of his meeting with Śrī Rāma beggars description.

When a loving devotee actually sees his beloved Lord, his eyelids refuse to fall. The impediment caused in the sight of the Lord even by the twinkling of his eyes becomes unbearable to him. The very twitching of eyelids is a great hindrance to him. Beholding the Lord with his eyes, touching His feet with his hands and hearing his dulcet voice with his ears, he drinks as it were the sweet nectar of His love. The unique loveliness and charm of his transcendent personality is beyond description. On the basis of the pen-pictures contained in the scriptures the Lord's personality is only faintly indicated. It is, however, not possible for a lover of the Lord to describe His personality while he is actually beholding it. He feels so enchanted at the sight that his speech itself begins to falter.

We read in the *Pātāla-Khaṇḍa* of the *Padma-Purāṇa* how,* when the Lord was returning from Laṅkā by air, Bharata on receiving His message by the mouth of Hanumān proceeded to receive Him and how, when the Lord saw him walking in the garb of an ascetic, clad in the bark of trees and wearing matted locks on his head, He forthwith got down from His aerial car, crying "Brother, brother" and repeating the word again and again. Tears of joy ran down his cheeks when Bharata saw the Lord alighting, and he fell prostrate on the ground. The Lord lifted him by his arms and clasped him to His bosom. Śrī Rāma

---

* यानादवततराशु विरहक्लिन्नमानसः ।
भ्रातर्भ्रातः पुनर्भ्रातर्भ्रातर्भ्रातर्वदन्मुहुः ॥

and Bharata both felt enraptured through love and the speech of both faltered.

Similarly, when a devotee is blessed with the sight of the Lord for the first time, his voice gets choked, his eyelids refuse to fall and he remains looking on with unwinking eyes. Then, when he returns to his normal self after some time, his mouth opens and he enters into conversation with the Lord. By the sight of the Lord all his doubts get cleared, the stock of his Karma gets depleted, and the knot of ignorance which links the soul with matter is resolved.

भिद्यते हृदयग्रन्थिश्छिद्यन्ते सर्वसंशयाः ।
क्षीयन्ते चास्य कर्माणि तस्मिन् दृष्टे परावरे ॥

(*Mundakopanisad* II.ii.8)

The feeling of identification with a material body, entertained by the conscious Spirit, or in other words the apparent unity of Matter and Spirit conceived through ignorance is what is meant by the knot of ignorance existing in the heart. This knot gets resolved through God-Realization. All doubts disappear and the entire stock of merit and sin attaching to him gets burnt. The devotee feels enchanted at the sight of the Lord and after that whatever he does is intended only to enrapture the Lord.

Śrī Rādhā represents the exhilarating energy of the Lord and all Her movements have the only motive of delighting and enrapturing the Lord. Every movement of the Lord too is likewise intended to enchant Śrī Rādhā. This effort on the part of both to gladden each other constitutes what is known as their amatory pastimes. These pastimes enhance the delight and intensify the love of each other, which ever grows from more to more. This sport of Rādhā and Kṛṣṇa is essentially a sport of love. Similarly all the movements of the devotee who has been blessed with the sight of his most beloved Lord, the only object of his love, are intended to gladden and enrapture the Lord; and all the movements of the Lord are likewise intended to delight and enchant His devotee. In this way both the lover and the Beloved try to enrapture and enchant each other. This loving sport of the devotee and his beloved Lord is transcendent in character. Their love is beyond description. Therefore, it is no exaggeration to say that neither the Lord nor His devotees can describe this loving pastime. Here it should be remembered that whereas the Lord is the Beloved in the eyes of the devotee, who is the lover, the devotee is the beloved in the eyes of the Lord, who plays the lover. The love they bear for each other is marvellous. Since they love each other on terms of equality, the feeling of esteem and reverence is absent. The love which is characterized by veneration and regard is also exalted; but so long as this feeling persists, the love falls short of the ideal. Where the two love each other on an equal footing, where there is unity, the question of superiority and inferiority does not arise. The devotee who is established in such unity really sports in the Lord, no matter what he does. The Lord says in the *Gītā*:—

सर्वभूतस्थितं यो मां भजत्येकत्वमास्थितः ।
सर्वथा वर्तमानोऽपि स योगी मयि वर्तते ॥

(VI.31)

"The Yogī who is established in unity with Me and worship Me as dwelling in all beings (as their very Self) stays in Me, no matter what he does."

An earlier stage of such unity is depicted in the following verse:—

यो मां पश्यति सर्वत्र सर्वं च मयि पश्यति ।
तस्याहं न प्रणश्यामि स च मे न प्रणश्यति ॥

(VI.30)

"He who sees Me (the Supreme Spirit) everywhere (wherever his mind goes, and in every object to which his eyes are directed), and everything as comprised in Me never loses sight of Me and I never lose sight of him (such a devotee keeps his eyes fixed on Me and I keep My eyes fixed on him)."

This transcendent amorous play goes on uninterrupted forever. The sense of pride and wounded pride are worldly (material) phenomena. Love transcends both.

During the period of striving, the devotee chants the Lord's name and hymns His praises. Nay, he feels enraptured when he understands the true significance, inwardness, excellences and glory of His name, personality, pastimes and divine abode, pays to Him his dutiful homage and respect and offers worship and formal service to Him. When, however, he transcends this stage and gets identified with the Lord, honour and praise, esteem and reverence or worship and attendance on either side become out of the question. Veneration and regard find their place only in the stage of Sādhanā. If I praise the Lord as the Redeemer of the fallen, it becomes evident that I am a sinner and that I hope to get purified because even the vilest sinner turns supremely holy and gets redeemed through His sight, by hearing His talk and by speaking to Him. When in affliction I would address the Lord as follows:—"Lord, You are an ocean of mercy ! Pray, take pity on me, who deserve Your compassion." This too is a very noble sentiment. Yet it falls outside the domain of love.

Similarly fear and shame have no place in the sphere of love; for they too figure in the stage of Sādhanā alone. The devotees of the Lord worship Him according to their respective attitude of mind. Where there exists the relation of husband and wife, the feeling of shame is absent but the sense of respect is there. A wife treats her husband with honour and respect and renders service to him. Where there is the relation of master and servant, the servant not only treats his master with honour and respect but also looks upon him with fear and feels shy in his presence. He cherishes a feeling of awe and reverence for his master. The feeling of parental affection is characterized by tenderness and accompanied by the sense of guardianship and fostering care. No such feeling is present in the attitude of oneness. In the attitude of friendship, of course, there is no sense of fear and infatuation either; mutual regard and veneration too are absent. But while there is no trace of shame and shyness in the relation of wife and husband, these do persist in some measure in the attitude of friendship. When a devotee transcends all these attitudes, shame and fear, honour and praise, respect and shyness, all disappear.

Our two hands become as one when united; but otherwise too there is no feeling of respect, fear or formality between them. Similarly when the devotee and the Lord meet, they become united. At the moment of union of the two even the garland, clothes and ornaments seem like separating elements. The blessed peace which is experienced through this loving union is different from that which results from the union with the Formless and Attributeless. In the latter there is no function; whereas in the former there is the divine Līlā or loving play. The devotee and the Lord do not turn their eyes from each other and their vision, speech, and touch at that time are all blissful, loving, ecstatic and sweet beyond expression. The Lord's figure appears to the devotee as full of bliss and made of nectar and the devotee's body for the Lord is the embodiment of devotion and full of bliss. Their talk is very sweet. The words are as sweet as nectar for the ears; and so are the vision and touch for the eyes and body respectively. Everything is blissful, loving and ecstatic. That experience can never be expressed in words. They seem to drink each other with their eyes and enter each other through touch. Their words are so sweet that they desire to hear them uninterruptedly and cannot suffer silence. The dropping of eyelids becomes unbearable as it obstructs the vision.

In this state the Lord and the devotee both become complete embodiments of the divine qualities or attributes, and the distinction between the attributes and the person to whom they belong vanishes. They transcend all attributes and attitudes of mind. The attributes of the Lord are divine by nature and He transcends even the Sattvic attributes which are the outcome of Māyā. For the moment the devotee also becomes the embodiment of the divine, transcendent attributes.

Really speaking, the lover, the beloved and the love subsisting between them are all one. God is the Beloved, devotee the lover and the relation they bear to each other is love. They may appear different but they are essentially one and are imbued with consciousness. In this realm of love none else can enter; and if one strays into it one cannot have the vision of the divine play. In that state there are no ornaments, no embellishments and no emblems either. Though the emblems and other appurtenances of the Lord are living and conscious, yet in that state of union none is required. Here devotion goes by the name of love and this union with or the attainment of the Lord is the highest achievement of the path of devotion, and in comparison to it even liberation is of little value. There is absolutely no trace of any kind of sensual enjoyment. This loving union between the Lord and the devotee is the highest form of Satsaṅga. And it is this which is highly praised in the *Rāmāyaṇa*—

तात स्वर्ग अपबर्ग सुख धरिय तुला एक अंग।
तूल न ताहि सकल मिलि जो सुख लव सतसंग ॥

"In one scale of the balance put together the delights of the heaven and the bliss of final beatitude; but they will all be outweighed by a moment's joy derived from Satsaṅga."

The Lord is Sat; it is one of His names. Therefore communion with Him or pure love for Him is called Satsaṅga. The delights of heaven and even the state of liberation stand nowhere when compared to it. And a devotee of this type is the highest kind of lover of the Divine. Contact with such a lover, meeting and talking to him lead to liberation.

The Lord granted liberation and a place in His own Abode to Pūtanā, the demoness who attempted to poison Him. Then what more could He give to Yaśodā, who put Him to her own breast and fed Him ? If final beatitude was the reward of both, that was no justice. It can be said in reply, "The Lord did grant liberation to Pūtanā but did not offer Himself to her as He surrendered Himself completely to Yaśodā by resting on her lap." It is a divine law that God offers Himself to the devotee who dedicates himself to Him. When the Lord gave Himself up to Yaśodā, then liberation was of no account to her. Final beatitude rolled in the dust of her courtyard. It is the belief of devotees that final beatitude dwells in the dust of Vraja. Then it can be easily conceded that it rolls in the dust of Yaśodā's courtyard. The idea is that whosoever puts it on his head or swallows it becomes entitled to get liberation.

Those great souls who are lost in the ecstasy of love are, really speaking, embodiments of love itself. Their contact fills others too with love and they freely communicate their devotional feeling to all and sundry.

When the Gopīs' beheld Lord Śrī Kṛṣṇa, covered all over with the dust raised by the hoofs of cows, returning to Vṛndāvana at sunset, they were lost in ecstasy. And this should cause no wonder to us when we remember that when Uddhava went to Vraja and witnessed the loving pastimes of the Gopīs' he was beside himself with joy and yearned to become some herb, creeper or vegetation, so that he might get the dust of the Gopīs' feet for his purification. When he returned to Lord Śrī Kṛṣṇa, who had sent him to teach Yoga and Jñāna to the Gopīs' he realized that on the pretence of sending him as a preceptor, the Lord had really sent him to receive instruction in Love from them. And this he declared before the Lord.

Those who have realized God always remain in blissful state. Their eyes betray the intoxication of love; and, losing themselves in love, they listlessly wander in the world. Even they who meet such a God-intoxicated person lose consciousness of external things or surroundings as well as of their own person. They lose sense even of their religious and social duties. When such a thing happens even during the practice of loving devotion, what follows on realizing God and becoming identified with Him is beyond description. How can anyone else describe what the Lord Himself cannot describe, as there is no expression for it ?

When we think of the Lord's compassion, it appears that He is an ocean of compassion. But this comparison too is derogatory, as the ocean has its limits while God's compassion is infinite. If all the compassion that mankind has were to be gathered together, it would not approximate even to a drop when compared to that vast ocean of compassion. Human compassion is nothing more than a Sattvic sentiment, while His compassion is divine and therefore beyond the three Guṇas. All human compassion is nothing more than a mere reflection of a drop of His compassion. The Lord's compassion is infinite and limitless. The sky may be conceived to have an end, but not His compassion. When man realizes that the Lord is so kind and merciful, then he understands the secret of mercy and love and he himself becomes a friend of all, and a loving and compassionate soul. And such a person cannot brook even a moment's separation from the Lord. His life becomes a burden without the Lord. And then it becomes impossible for him to live without the Lord, because he realizes that He is extremely kind and merciful; He is present everywhere, and is always eager to meet those who have firm faith in Him and are devoted to Him. Gosvāmī Tulasīdāsa says in his *Rāmacaritamānasa*—

आकर चारि लाख चौरासी।
जोनि भ्रमत यह जिव अबिनासी॥
फिरत सदा माया कर प्रेरा।
काल कर्म सुभाव गुन घेरा॥
कबहुँक करि करुना नर देही।
देत ईस बिनु हेतु सनेही॥

"This immortal soul goes round through eighty-four lakh species of life, falling under four broad divisions. Driven by Māyā and encompassed by Time, Destiny, Nature and Phenomenal existence, it ever drifts along. Rarely does God, who loves the Jīva without any self-interest, graciously bestow on it a human form."

We never deserved to be invested with a human form; He bestowed it upon us out of compassion. He did so only because it is man who can understand that God loves him out of kindness and without any self-interest. If man fails to understand this, God's purpose remains unfulfilled. We are designated as human beings and so should not be devoid of the feeling of gratitude towards the Lord and forget His divine qualities and benevolence. The *Gītā* also says that the Lord does good to us without any selfish interest of His own

सुहृदं सर्वभूतानां ज्ञात्वा मां शान्तिमृच्छति ।

"Having known Me as the disinterested friend of all beings, My devotee attains peace."

Thus the Lord is kind to us without any self-interest of His own. And if still we do not get supreme and abiding peace, it means we have not understood His nature. One who realizes the compassionate nature of the Lord is filled with such transcendent peace and joy that one forgets oneself. And then one becomes a friend of all. Describing the characteristics of His devotees, the Lord says—

अद्वेष्टा सर्वभूतानां मैत्रः करुण एव च ।

"He is free from malice towards all beings and is friendly and compassionate as well."

If we come to know the secret of the Lord's compassionate nature, we can also become compassionate towards all. If we do not profit by this principle it should be a matter of shame and painful sorrow for us. It is our foolishness and ignorance which are responsible for our lack of faith in the principle. We should, however, do our utmost to understand the secret of the Lord's compassion. Firmness of faith will automatically bring Him within our easy reach.

The Lord is always earnest and eager to meet us. But we should have full faith in this. When once we realize that with extended arms He, so affectionate and kind, is ever ready to meet us, then we too cannot live without Him for a moment. Such a feeling should always be kept alive in our heart and we should grow restless to meet Him.

When a child becomes impatient and restless to meet his mother, she kindly takes it in her embrace. The Lord is infinitely more compassionate than any mother. Only if we realized this fact our eagerness to meet Him would be so poignant that unless He gathered us in His arms our wailing would not cease. The Lord marks only our earnestness, eagerness, faith, love and impatience. Knowing this if we get immersed in God-consciousness there can be no delay in our meeting Him. When the electric installation is completed, and connection obtained, you press the button and instantly there is light. Similarly when we become fit for God-Realization, we attain to His presence the moment we are filled with God-consciousness.

★

Means of Developing Love for God

People seeking God-Realization should strive hard to develop a distaste for the world and love for God. There are many an obstacle in the path of self-discipline, such as lack of concentration, sloth, luxury and carelessness. Of these, again, lack of concentration and sloth are the two main obstacles. When one develops a distaste for the world and love for God, all these obstacles automatically disappear. Hence what is needed is a strenuous endeavour for cultivating a distaste for the world and love for God.

To look upon the world as transient, ephemeral, consisting of sorrow, loathsome, detrimental to one's best interests and a source of terror; to cultivate the fellowship of persons who are established in dispassion; to read books inculcating dispassion and to draw pictures of dispassion before the mind—these are the means for developing a distaste for the world.

To hear, read and ponder dissertations on the virtues, glory, essence and secret of the Lord's names, personality, pastimes and abode; to cultivate the fellowship of those cherishing love for the Lord; to glorify and offer prayers to the Lord with a guileless heart, in a pathetic spirit and in a voice choked with emotion; to realize one's eternal relation with the Lord—to look upon Him as one's own and oneself as His own; to visualize the presence of the Lord and speak to Him touch His divine person and hold conversation with Him, fix one's thought on Him and dwell on His name and personality in a disinterested spirit all the time—these are the means of developing love for the Lord. One can achieve palpable success by practising all these means with faith and reverence.

When a striver develops a distaste for the world and love for God, all his weaknesses in the shape of evil propensities, immorality, impure addictions, excessive thought of the world, sloth, error, craving for enjoyment and so on get eliminated; nay true realization of God comes to him and even-mindedness appears in him as a matter of course. Noble traits then manifest themselves of their own accord and all his activities become ideal. He continues at every time to enjoy supreme peace and highest bliss. The result is that such a man does not give himself over to luxuries and evil company even if he finds himself in such surroundings.

In order to adopt the aforesaid means one should devote particular attention to the following three suggestions:—

(1) While retiring at night, let us go to bed with our thought fixed on the Lord's name, personality, excellences and glory. By doing so, we shall not have bad dreams and our period of sleep too may be included in our period of striving.

(2) While doing our work during the daytime we should feel that whatever we are doing is God's work alone and that we are doing it as a behest of God and for His sake; that the whole of this creation, animate as well as inanimate, belongs to God and we too are His; nay, that God is ours and pervades all, so that service rendered to all is service rendered to Him alone. And in our dealing with others we should be particularly careful to see that they are characterized by a spirit of self-abnegation, benevolence, magnanimity, even-mindedness and natural compassion towards all living beings. In this way our dealings with others naturally begin to be noble.

A still more exalted feeling is the sentiment of the man all whose actions are free from egotism and pride, who feels that whatever is done by him is inspired by the Lord and that he is a mere instrument in His hands. An action inspired by such sentiment has absolutely no chance of being actuated by an evil propensity or characterized by immorality and so on. If it is prompted by an evil propensity or bad habit, or characterized by immorality, it should be taken for granted that it is not God-inspired, but inspired by lust. When Arjuna put the following question to the Lord—

अथ केन प्रयुक्तोऽयं पापं चरति पूरुषः ।
अनिच्छन्नपि वार्ष्णेय बलादिव नियोजितः ॥

(III.36)

"Now impelled by what, O Krsna, does this man commit sin even involuntarily, as though driven by force ?"

He replied as follows:—

काम एष क्रोध एष रजोगुणसमुद्भवः ।
महाशनो महापाप्मा विद्ध्येनमिह वैरिणम् ॥

(III.37)

"It is desire begotten of the element of Rajas, which appears as wrath; nay, it is insatiable and grossly wicked. Know this to be the enemy in this case."

Even while going through a course of spiritual discipline in seclusion one ought to control one's mind and senses in the first instance. Continued effort at concentration and dispassion alone are the principal means of subjugating the mind and senses. The Lord says in the *Gītā:—*

असंशयं महाबाहो मनो दुर्निग्रहं चलम् ।
अभ्यासेन तु कौन्तेय वैराग्येण च गृह्यते ॥

(VI.35)

"The mind is restless no doubt, and difficult to curb, O Arjuna; but it can be brought under control by repeated practice (of meditation) and by the exercise of dispassion, O son of Kuntī !"

The mind having been controlled, the subjugation of the senses is already accomplished as a part of the aforesaid process.

When the mind has been controlled, one should take to the practice of turning one's mind towards His name and personality with reverence and love; for any course of spiritual discipline is not easy to pursue for one who has not been able to control one's mind and spiritual discipline is helpful in enabling one to realize God.

The Lord says:—

असंयतात्मना योगो दुष्प्राप इति मे मतिः ।
वश्यात्मना तु यतता शक्योऽवाप्तुमुपायतः ॥

(*Gītā* VI.36)

"Yoga is difficult of achievement for one whose mind is not subdued; by him, however, who has the mind under control, and is ceaselessly striving, it can be easily attained through practice. Such is My conviction."

Later on the Lord declares the discipline of Devotion in the form of reverent adoration of and contemplation on the Lord as the best of all.

योगिनामपि सर्वेषां मद्गतेनान्तरात्मना ।
श्रद्धावान् भजते यो मां स मे युक्ततमो मतः ॥

(*Gītā* VI.47)

"Of all Yogīs, again, he who devoutly worships Me with his mind focussed on Me is considered by Me to be the best Yogī."

Or one should sit in a lonely place, give up all desires, subdue one's senses with the help of the mind and, dead to the world, fix one's mind on God. This too is an excellent means of God-Realization. The Lord Himself says in the *Gītā*:—

संकल्पप्रभवान् कामांस्त्यक्त्वा सर्वानशेषतः ।
मनसैवेन्द्रियग्रामं विनियम्य समन्ततः ॥
शनैः शनैरुपरमेद् बुद्ध्या धृतिगृहीतया ।
आत्मसंस्थं मनः कृत्वा न किंचिदपि चिन्तयेत् ॥

(VI.24-25)

"Completely renouncing all desires arising from thoughts of the world, and fully restraining the whole pack of the senses from all sides by the mind, he should through gradual practice attain tranquillity; and fixing the mind on God through reason controlled by steadfastness, he should not think of anything else. Drawing back the restless and fidgety mind from all those objects after which it runs, he should repeatedly fix in on God."

Therefore, in order to surmount all worldly obstacles and attain God-Realization, one should strive hard to cultivate dispassion and develop love for God.

Lights on Love for God and Devotion

The Mind of a Devotee that has Taken Refuge in God Prays to Him:—

O Sustainer of the universe, O Commiserator of the afflicted, O Purifier of the fallen, O Almighty Lord, O Befriender of the meek, O Nārāyaṇa, O Hari, pray, have mercy on me. Be gracious to me. O Inner Controller of all, you are well-known in the world by the epithet 'Ocean of mercy.' Hence it is but natural for you to shower Your grace on me.

O Lord, if You enjoy the title of "Purifier of the fallen," be good enough to appear before me at least once. Prostrating myself before You again and again, I implore You to bless me with Your sight. O Lord ! Other than You in this world there is none whom I can call my own. Be pleased, therefore, to show Your countenance to me, to reveal Yourself before me. Tantalize me no more. You go by the name of Viśvambhara (Sustainer of the universe). Why, then, do You not grant my hope ? By showing grace to me Your stock of mercy will not grow less in any measure. An iota of Your mercy is capable of redeeming the whole world. Of what account is it, then, for You to redeem an insignificant creature like me ? If You take into account the record of my doings, there can be no hope whatsoever of my being freed from the trammels of mundane existence. Therefore, pray, recall Your own title of "Patita-Pāvana" (The Purifier of the fallen) and bless this insignificant creature with Your sight. I know nothing either of Devotion or of Yoga or of any ritual by virtue of which I may hope to be blessed with Your sight. Be pleased, therefore, O Lord ! To manifest Yourself before me but once.

The Jīvātmā (Embodied Soul) Twits the Mind as Follows:—

"O wicked mind ! Can the Lord, who is the Inner Controller of all, be propitiated through a deceitful prayer ? Is He not aware that all these entreaties of yours are not being made in a disinterested spirit and that you have no iota of faith, reverence or love in your heart ? If you really believe that God is our Inner Controller, wherefore do you pray (to Him) ? The Lord never listens to a sham prayer devoid of love. And if you cherish love in your heart, your prayer is superfluous. For the Lord Himself says in the *Gītā*—

ये यथा मां प्रपद्यन्ते तांस्तथैव भजाम्यहम् ॥

(IV.11)

"Howsoever men seek Me, even so do I approach them."

ये भजन्ति तु मां भक्त्या मयि ते तेषु चाप्यहम् ।

(IX.29)

"They, however, who devoutly worship Me dwell in Me, and I too stand revealed in them."*

O my mind ! Even if Śrī Hari, in spite of His being an ocean of compassion, withholds His mercy, you need not worry. What we are required to do is to go on performing our duty. Śrī Hari is an ideal lover; He cognizes true love. A lover alone knows the secret of love. Can that Indweller of all hearts reveal Himself before you through your insipid love ? When the cord of unalloyed love and genuine faith and reverence gets ready, Śrī Hari will be automatically drawn into your presence by that cord. O foolish mind, a false prayer will not be of any avail to you. For Śrī Hari indwells all hearts. O my mind, I bow to you. It is your wont to revolve in the world. So sally forth whithersoever you like. It is due to your fellowship that I continued to revolve in this unsubstantial world so long. Now by taking refuge in the lotus feet of Śrī Hari I have been able to see through your wiles. You plead with the Lord for my sake with a false show of devotion and in a most pitiful language; but you are not aware that Śrī Hari indwells all hearts. The author of the *Yogavāsiṣṭha* rightly says that until and unless the mind is divested of its vagrancy or gets

* Even as a fire, though present everywhere in a subtle form, is manifested only through combustible substances, so God, though pervading everywhere, visibly manifests Himself only in the mind of a man worshipping Him with devotion.

extinct it is not possible to realize God. Eradication of desire, extinction of the mind and God-Realization take place synchronously. Therefore I beseech you to withdraw honourably. The bird of my soul has no longer any chance of being caught in your snare; for it has taken shelter in the feet of Śrī Hari. Are you going to clear away only after being subjected to abject humiliation ? Oh, where is that Māyā ? Whither have my enemies in the shape of lust, anger and so on fled ? Now the whole of your army is dwindling. Hence giving up all hope of casting your spell on me, you may go wherever you like.

The Mind prays to the Lord again:—

"O Lord, my Master, be propitious to me ! I am entirely at Your mercy. O Protector of those who come to You for protection, save the honour of this servant who has sought You for protection. O Lord, save me. O ! Come to my rescue. Be pleased to manifest Yourself before me only once. I have no support other than You in this world. It is therefore that I bow to You, prostrate myself before You again and again. Pray, do not tarry; bless me with Your sight speedily. O ! Ocean of mercy, enquire after my welfare once. If You fail to come, no prop will be left for my life. O Lord, take pity on me, be gracious to me. Regard me with an eye of compassion once. O ! Befriender of the afflicted, O ! commiserator of the humble, take no notice of my wickedness and demonstrate Your character as the Purifier of the fallen.

The Jīvātmā Admonishes the Mind once more:—

O My mind, be cautious and forewarned ! Why do you rave in vain ? Śrī Hari—who is Truth, Consciousness and Bliss solidified—does not want a false prayer. Your wiles will not succeed any more in my case. I do not want any such prayer from you.

If Śrī Hari is the Witness of all hearts, where lies the need of offering prayers to Him ? If He is a lover, what is the need of calling Him ? If He is the Sustainer of the universe, what is the necessity of asking Him for anything ?

The Jīvātmā now addresses his Intellect and senses

O my senses, you flourish only where there is a craving for

pleasure. I have taken refuge in the feet of Śrī Hari; hence there is no scope for you. O my intellect, your wisdom took leave of you when you exhorted me to get lost in the maize of this world. That exhortation of yours will not have any effect on me now.

The Jīvātmā then turns towards God and prays:—

O Lord, since You are the witness of all hearts, I do not implore You to bless me with Your sight; for, had my heart overflowed with love for You, would it be possible for You to tarry any longer ? Would it be possible even for Mother Lakṣmī to detain You ? Nay, had I developed full reverence for You, could You have delayed Your visit to me ? Could that love and reverence have let You remain behind ? Oh, in vain do I pose as a disinterested and desireless person in this world and in vain do I consider myself as one who has sought You as one's protector. But there is nothing to be worried about. I should remain gratified with whatever comes to me. For so have You taught in the *Gītā*.* Therefore, if in the course of my remaining absorbed in loving devotion to Your lotus feet I get an abode in hell, I would prefer it to heaven. Under such circumstances I have nothing to worry about. When I develop love for You, will it not evoke love in You too ? When I am no longer able to live without Your sight, will it be possible for You to do without seeing me ? You have Yourself observed in the *Gītā*:—

ये यथा मां प्रपद्यन्ते तांस्तथैव भजाम्यहम्।

"Howsoever men seek Me, even so do I approach them."

That is why I do not ask You to bless me with Your sight and You too care little to see me. But I am not at all worried on that score; You may do as You deem fit. I should feel delighted with whatever You do.

Transported with joy while Gazing on the Lord with His Mental eyes, the Jīvātmā Exclaims:—

Ah, what a joy ! How blissful ! Hurrah ! O Lord, my Master,

---

* यदृच्छालाभसंतुष्टः (IV.22)
and संतुष्टो येन केनचित् (XII.19)

have You come ? How blessed, how lucky I am ! Even I, a fallen creature, have attained my goal today by the grace of Your lotus feet ! There is no wonder that it should be so. For You have Yourself proclaimed in the *Gītā:*—

अपि चेत् सुदुराचारो भजते मामनन्यभाक् ।
साधुरेव स मन्तव्यः सम्यग्व्यवसितो हि सः ॥
क्षिप्रं भवति धर्मात्मा शश्वच्छान्तिं निगच्छति ।
कौन्तेय प्रति जानीहि न मे भक्तः प्रणश्यति ॥

(IX.30-31)

"Even if the vilest fellow worships Me with exclusive devotion, he should be accounted a saint; for he has rightly resolved. (He is positive in his belief that there is nothing like devoted worship of God.)

Speedily he becomes virtuous and secures lasting peace. Know it for certain, Arjuna, that My devotee never falls."

While visualizing the Marvellous Personality of God, the Jīvātmā mentally dilates upon his comeliness as follows:—

Oh, how lovely are the Lord's feet, glowing like two small heaps of sapphires and possessing the brilliance of numberless suns. How tender are His toes crowned with bright nails at the outer extremities ! The ankles are adorned with anklets of gold. Like His lotus feet His knees, shanks and other limbs too are shining through His loin-cloth of silk like so many other heaps of sapphires. Oh, how charming are His four shapely arms, adorned with precious jewels like armlets and bangles, the upper two carrying a conch and a discus and the lower two holding a mace and a lotus ! Oh, how bewitching is His bosom, the middle of which is distinguished by the presence of His divine Spouse, Goddess Lakṣmī (in the form of a golden streak) and a footprint of the sage Bhṛgu ! How attractive is His conch-like neck, decked with necklaces of gold, pearls and precious stones and the Kaustubha gem as well as with a Vaijayantī and other garlands ! The Lord is possessed of a beautiful chin, ruddy lips and a most enchanting nose, the tip of which is set off with a pearl. The

Lord's eyes are as big as a pair of full-blown lotuses. His ears are adorned with alligator-shaped ear-rings made of precious stones; His forehead bears a Tilaka (a sacred mark) and a crown inlaid with precious stones adorns His head. Ah, the Lord's globular countenance resembles the full moon and stands invested with a circle of rays resembling the rays of the sun, which irradiate the jewels of His crown and ornaments ! Oh, I am blessed indeed. How fortunate am I that I am standing face to face with the all-blissful Śrī Hari, who is wearing a gentle smile on His blooming countenance !

Overwhelmed with joy, the Jīvātmā thus beholds with his mental eyes at a distance of a cubit and a quarter before him the supreme Deity standing in the air a cubit and a quarter above the ground in the form of a tender youth of twelve, and offers worship to Him mentally as follows:—

The Procedure of Mental Worship

१. पादयोः पाद्यं समर्पयामि नारायणाय नमः ।

Reciting the above formula, he washes with pure water the lotus feet of the Lord and sprinkles his head with the water thus consecrated with the touch of those sacred feet.

२. हस्तयोरर्घ्यं समर्पयामि नारायणाय नमः ।

So saying, he pours pure water in the hollow of the Lord's palms so as to enable Him to wash them.

३. आचमनीयं समर्पयामि नारायणाय नमः ।

Uttering the above words, he offers to the Lord water to rinse His mouth with (and thus refresh Himself).

४. गन्धं समर्पयामि नारायणाय नमः ।

With these words on his lips he paints the Lord's forehead with sandal-paste as an auspicious mark.

५. मुक्ताफलं समर्पयामि नारायणाय नमः ।

Reciting the above formula, he fixes a pearl at the centre of the Lord's forehead with the help of the sandal-paste by way of adornment.

६. पुष्पाणि समर्पयामि नारायणाय नमः ।

With the above words on his lips he showers flowers on the head of the Lord by way of greeting.

७. मालां समर्पयामि नारायणाय नमः ।

Uttering the above words, he places a garland round the Lord's neck by way of adornment and as a mark of respect.

८. धूपमाघ्रापयामि नारायणाय नमः ।

Saying so, he burns incense to the Lord in order to perfume and purify the air round Him.

९. दीपं दर्शयामि नारायणाय नमः ।

Reciting the above formula, he kindles a light in the shape of a wick of cotton soaked with ghee and shows it to the Lord.

१०. नैवेद्यं समर्पयामि नारायणाय नमः ।

Uttering the above words, he offers dainty dishes to the Lord by way of repast.

११. आचमनीयं समर्पयामि नारायणाय नमः ।

Saying so, he offers to the Lord water to rinse His mouth with.

१२. ऋतुफलानि समर्पयामि नारायणाय नमः ।

With the above words on his lips he offers seasonal fruits to the Lord by way of desserts.

१३. पुनराचमनीयं समर्पयामि नारायणाय नमः ।

Reciting the above formula, he offers to the Lord water to rinse His mouth with once more.

१४. पूगीफलं सताम्बूलं समर्पयामि नारायणाय नमः ।

Uttering the above words, he offers betel-leaves with areca-nut parings and cardamoms etc., to the Lord in order to perfume His mouth.

१५. पुनराचमनीयं समर्पयामि नारायणाय नमः ।

Saying so, he offers to the Lord water to rinse His mouth with for a third time. Igniting a lump of a camphor in a gold plate, he then waves lights before the Lord.

१६. पुष्पाञ्जलिं समर्पयामि नारायणाय नमः ।

With the above words on his lips he takes flowers in the hollow of his palms and showers them on the Lord.

Then, going round the Lord clockwise as a mark of respect four times, he falls prostrate before Him by way of humble submission.

× × × ×

After offering worship mentally to the Lord as indicated above, the Jīvātmā lays Him down to rest in the cavity of his heart and, dwelling with his mind on His divine personality and innumerable excellences, bows his head to Him time and again with the following verse on his lips—

शान्ताकारं भुजगशयनं पद्मनाभं सुरेशं
विश्वाधारं गगनसदृशं मेघवर्णं शुभाङ्गम् ।
लक्ष्मीकान्तं कमलनयनं योगिभिर्ध्यानगम्यं
वन्दे विष्णुं भवभयहरं सर्वलोकैकनाथम् ॥

"I bow to Lord Viṣṇu of blessed limbs, the Supreme Ruler of the gods, the Beloved of Lakṣmī (the goddess of beauty and prosperity), who wears a most serene aspect, uses the serpentgod (Śeṣa) for His bed, has a lotus sprung from His navel, is the Sustainer of the universe and all-pervading as ether, possesses the hue of a cloud and lotus-like eyes, is accessible to the Yogīs through meditation, dispels the fear of transmigration and is the one Protector of all the worlds."

He further extols the Lord as follows:—

"I bow repeatedly to Lord Śrī Hari who possesses the brilliance of countless suns, the coolness of numberless moons, the glow of millions of fires, the prowess of innumerable windgods, the glory of countless Indras, the comeliness of millions of Cupids, the forbearance of numberless earths, the profundity of millions of oceans, nay who is beyond all comparison, whose real character has only been speculated upon and could not be ascertained by the Vedas and other scriptures."

"I bow again and again to Lord Śrī Viṣṇu", the Purifier of the fallen, who is Truth, Consciousness and Bliss personified, who incessantly wears a gentle smile on His bright countenance and is

adorned with sparkling drops of perspiration all over His body !"

* * * *

Mentally fanning Śrī Hari and kneading His soles, the Jīvātmā now extols Him as follows:—

O Lord ! You alone are Brahmā (the Creator); You alone are Viṣṇu; You alone are the great god Śiva; You alone are the sun; the moon and other heavenly bodies; You alone are the three spheres known by the names of Bhūḥ (the terrestrial world), Bhuvaḥ (the aerial region) and Svaḥ (the heavenly world). Nay, the fourteen spheres as well as the seven Dvīpas or divisions of the terrestrial region—in short, all objective existence is Your own manifestation. You alone are the Cosmic Being; You alone are Hiraṇyagarbha (the subtle body of Brahmā); You alone are the four-armed Nārāyaṇa; nay, You alone are the stainless Brahma (the Absolute), beyond the taint of Māyā. It is You who have assumed countless forms; hence the entire creation is Your manifestation alone. Nay, the perceiver, that which is perceived and the act of perception—all these are You. Therefore:—

नमः समस्तभूतानामादिभूताय भूभृते ।
अनेकरूपरूपाय विष्णवे प्रभविष्णवे ॥

"Hail to You, the all-pervading Lord, the Origin of all created beings, the Sustainer of the earth, appearing in endless forms from aeon to aeon."

त्वमेव माता च पिता त्वमेव त्वमेव बन्धुश्च सखा त्वमेव ।
त्वमेव विद्या द्रविणं त्वमेव त्वमेव सर्वं मम देवदेव ॥

"You alone are the mother and You alone are the father. You alone are my relation and You alone are my friend. You alone are my learning, You alone are my wealth. You alone are my all, O god of gods !"

When a man thus pursuing loving devotion to God develops excessive fondness for Him, he loses consciousness even of his body etc. Of such a soul, the celebrated saint Sundaradāsa says:—

"When a man develops attachment to the Supreme Lord, he forgets all about his home and hearth. He roams here and there and

*no longer retains the least consciousness of his body. He heaves deep sighs and experiences a thrill of joy, tears streaming from his eyes incessantly. Nay, drinking to his fill the cup of love, he gets intoxicated. Who is, then, to practise the nine types of formal Devotion prescribed in the scriptures ?"**

"Such a man no longer cares for the opinion of the three worlds nor does he strictly follow the injunctions of the Vedas. He is little afraid of spirits and genii nor does he entertain the least fear of gods and demigods. He gives ear to none and refuses to look at anyone, nor does he crave for anything. And he utters no word with his lips. Such are the characteristics of loving Devotion."†

"Drunk with love, he roams about uttering incoherent words. One cherishing love for the Lord ought to long for Him intensely, forgetting one's very self even as the cowherdesses of Vraja did."‡

"How can a man have peace of mind without finding a remedy for his anguish, feeling miserable as he does like a fish without water or like a babe without the mother's breast ? He finds charm nowhere, who hankers for the Lord as fondly as the Cātaka bird longs for a rain-drop on the day when the asterism Svātī (Arcturus) is in the ascendant or the Cakora bird for the moon or even as a snake pines for a sandal-wood tree, a pauper for wealth or a lover for his beloved. Such is the way of love and where there is love there can be no room for stringency. So does Sundaradāsa speak of love."§

---

* प्रेम लग्यो परमेस्वर सों, तब भूलि गयो सिगरो घरबारा।
ज्यों उन्मत्त फिरै जित-ही-तित, नैक, रही न सरीर-सँभारा॥
स्वास उसास, उठे सब रोम, चलै दृग नीर अखंडित धारा।
सुंदर कौन करै नवधा बिधि, छाकि पर्‌यो रस पी मतवारा॥

† न लाज तीन लोक की, न बेद को कह्यो करै।
न संक भूत प्रेत की, न देव-जच्छ तें डरै॥
सुनै न कान और की, द्रसै न और इच्छ ना।
कहै न मुक्ख और बात, भक्ति प्रेम-लच्छना॥

‡ प्रेम अधीनो छाक्यो डोलै, क्यूँ की क्यूँ ही बानी बोलै। जैसे गोपी भूली देहा, तैसो चाहे जासों नेहा॥

§ नीर बिनु मीन दुखी, छीर बिनु सिसु जैसे, पीर की ओषधि बिनु, कैसे रह्यो जात है॥
चातक ज्यों स्वाति बूँद, चंद को चकोर जैसे, चंदन की चाह करि सर्प अकुलात है॥
निर्धन ज्यों धन चाहै, कामिनी को कंत चाहै, ऐसी जाके चाह ताहि, कछु न सुहात है॥
प्रेमको प्रवाह ऐसो, प्रेम तहाँ नेम कैसो, सुंदर कहत यह प्रेम ही की बात है॥

*"Now he laughs and, springing on his feet, begins to dance in joy; and now he starts crying as a babe. Now his voice gets choked and he is no more able to speak. Sometimes he goes into raptures and starts singing at the pitch of his voice; while at other times he sits mute and uncovered. When the mind gets absorbed in Śrī Hari, how can a man remain in his senses ? Says Sundaradāsa "Such are the outward marks of loving Devotion; hark you, my disciple"**

× × × ×

When the personality of the Lord disappears from his view, the Jīvātmā gets merged in the all-pervading Brahma, the Supreme Spirit, which is Truth, Consciousness and Bliss solidified, and exclaims:—

"Oh, the joy of it ! How blissful !! What extreme felicity !!! The one Vāsudeva† is everywhere. Oh, bliss alone pervades the entire space."

No lust, no anger, no greed, no infatuation, no arrogance, no jealousy, no pride, no agitation, no Māyā, no mind, no reason, no senses. A composite of Truth, Consciousness and Bliss alone exists everywhere. Ah, there is one self existent, all-conscious, impenetrable, all-perfect, immutable, undecaying, unmanifest, unthinkable, eternal, indescribable, everlasting, omnipresent, immovable, constant, imperceptible, intangible joy, supreme bliss, infinite bliss, bliss and bliss alone, bliss that is beyond Māyā reigning everywhere. There is nothing else than bliss. Oṁ ! Peace ! Peace !! Peace !!!

═══★═══

* कबहुक हँसि उठि नृत्य करै रोवन फिर लागे। कबहुँक गदगद कंठ, सब्द निकसै नहिं आगे॥
कबहुँक हृदय उमंग, बहुत ऊँचे स्वर गावै। कबहुँक ह्वै मुख मौन, गगन ऐसे रहि जावै॥
चित्त वित्त हरि सों लग्यो, सावधान कैसे रहै। यह प्रेम-लच्छना भक्ति है, सिष्य सुनहु सुंदर कहै॥

† The Gītā says—

बहूनां जन्मनामन्ते ज्ञानवान् मां प्रपद्यते। वासुदेवः सर्वमिति स महात्मा सुदुर्लभः॥

(VII.19)

"In the very last of all births the enlightened soul worships Me, realizing that all this is God, such a great soul is very rare."

Blessedness through Supreme Service

Generally speaking, all living beings in the world are steeped in suffering. Suffering is of two kinds—(1) worldly and (2) Other-worldly. Worldly suffering again is of three varieties—(1) that inflicted by other created beings such as birds and beasts, insects and reptiles and so on; (2) that brought about by the divine agencies or deities presiding over wind, fire, water, rain, space, time, constellations, the sun, the moon, etc., and (3) ailment of body or mind. There are two varieties of mental distemper too, *viz.*, (1) diseases like feebleness of mind and intellect, epilepsy, insanity, hysteria etc., and (2) evil propensities like lust, anger, greed, infatuation, arrogance, jealousy, partiality and prejudice, envy and fear, chicanery and deceit, etc., that are prejudicial to one's spiritual well-being. And maladies affecting the body and the organs of sense constitute bodily distemper. Other-worldly suffering implies peregrination of the soul in the other world after death or even in this world by being reborn in various species of life. Sufferings of all these types are completely brought to an end only through real knowledge of God. It is through such knowledge, again, that one comes to realize God. When God is realized one is finally rid of sorrows and sufferings of all the above-mentioned categories and attains supreme peace and transcendent joy. Although the body of even a God-realized soul may be undergoing the above-noted sufferings as a result of Prārabdha or evil destiny in the eyes of the people, yet his soul is beyond all suffering as a matter of fact. Morbidities like partiality and prejudice, joy and grief etc., disappear once for all in him and his soul ceases to have any connection with the body and senses—internal as well as external. Hence bodily sufferings brought about by his evil destiny are of no account. Such a true knowledge of God is attained through devotion to Him, fellowship with saints, study of scriptures like the *Gītā* and disinterested action, and by undergoing the disciplines of meditation and spiritual enlightenment etc., as detailed in the *Gītā*. Out of these the topic of disinterested action inspired by devotion to God is partially dealt with below.

The glorious Lord exists in all living beings. Therefore service rendered to one's fellow-beings is service to God, says the *Gītā*:—

यतः प्रवृत्तिर्भूतानां येन सर्वमिदं ततम्।
स्वकर्मणा तमभ्यर्च्य सिद्धिं विन्दति मानवः॥

(XVIII.46)

"Man attains the highest perfection by worshipping through his own natural duties Him from whom the tide of creation has streamed forth and by whom all this universe is pervaded."

Such service is rendered as a matter of course by those who have attained perfection. For the striver, of course, the virtues and conduct of such perfect souls serves as a goal. Keeping before his eyes the virtues and conduct of such men as their ideal, a striver should, therefore, try to follow them. The characteristics of such perfect and loving devotees have been described by the Lord in verses 13 to 19 of discourse XII of the *Gītā*, and those that walk in their footsteps have been declared by the Lord as surpassingly dear to Him.

ये तु धर्म्यामृतमिदं यथोक्तं पर्युपासते।
श्रद्दधाना मत्परमा भक्तास्तेऽतीव मे प्रियाः॥

(XII.20)

"Those devotees, however, who fully partake in a disinterested way of this nectar of pious wisdom set forth above, endowed with faith and solely devoted to Me, they are extremely dear to Me."

Therefore, viewing God as pervading all and keeping in mind His name and form, one should render service to all in a disinterested spirit according to His commandments. Such service can be classed under two heads—(1); service and (2) supreme service.

'Service' consists in alleviating the suffering of and gratifying those men and women who are feeling miserable, helpless and distressed on account of suffering caused by an earthquake, flood, famine, fire etc., due to illness or any other trouble.

There are several ways of rendering worldly service, as for example:—

(1) To arrange personally or through others for the food and clothing, medicine or any other kind of treatment and prescribed diet etc., with respect to an ailing or distressed person lying on the roadside without food, clothing or medical treatment, after getting him admitted into a hospital or lodging him anywhere else. Service rendered to the destitutes, poor and ailing who have none to look after them is indeed most praiseworthy. Hence, everyone of us should undertake such service. Doctors or Vaidyas working in charitable dispensaries, or rendering gratuitous service should make it a rule not to charge any fee even from the patients whom they visit at the latters' residence, much less from those who call on them at the dispensary itself.

(2) To arrange personally or through others for the food, clothing and shelter of one whose house and other belongings have been burnt by fire or washed away by flood and who has been rendered homeless or left without any means of subsistence or covering.

(3) To arrange personally or through others for food and lodging etc., of those who have lost their house and all other property in an earthquake, whose wife and children have been buried under debris or of such women and children who have become masterless.

(4) To arrange for the food and clothing as well as for the education etc., of minor boys and girls who have lost their parents and are left without guardian by getting them admitted into an orphanage or elsewhere.

(5) To help personally according to one's means or through others a person who is unable to marry his or her daughter due to poverty.

(6) To arrange personally or through others for the food and clothing etc., of a widow without any provision for such bare necessaries of life.

Apart from the widowed mothers and sisters in indigent families, who are finding it hard these days to get even their daily bread and to keep their body and soul together, many widows of well-to-do houses too are not being honourably treated in their own husband's or father's house. They appear as a veritable burden to the other inmates of their house who have no reverence or regard for them. That is why they are despised everywhere. If these widows deposit in their husband's or father's house whatever ornaments or cash they happen to possess, there are some who usurp their all. This has been observed in many cases. Therefore widowed mothers and sisters are advised to convert their valuables into hard cash and get it deposited in bank or get debentures for the said money even though they fetch a small interest.

Widowed mothers and sisters are requested to spend their time, like those who are free from worldly attachment, in the pursuit of knowledge, dispassion and good morals as well as in Devotion to God consisting of adoration and meditation etc., as also in austerities in the form of restraining the mind and the senses. Besides, the most useful thing for them is to render disinterested service to all the inmates of their husband's or father's house in the form of cooking and sewing etc. It is forbidden for them to take their meals without lending a helping hand in the household work. If they work in a spirit of selfless service as aforesaid, not only will their mind get purified but the people of their husband's or father's house will also remain pleased. The foremost duty of a widow is to practise Japa, meditation and study of the scriptures etc., in a secluded place both morning and evening, to go to sleep at bed-time with her mind fixed on the name and form, excellences and glory of God, and even during the hours of working—to cultivate the habit of working in a selfless spirit for the pleasure of God regarding all work as His and remembering Him all the time. The Lord says in the *Gītā*—

तस्मात् सर्वेषु कालेषु मामनुस्मर युध्य च ।
मय्यर्पितमनोबुद्धिर्मामेवैष्यस्यसंशयम् ॥

(VIII.7)

"Therefore, Arjuna, think of Me at all times and fight. With mind and reason thus set on Me, you will doubtless come to Me."

Similarly, other men and women too should not only treat the widowed mothers and sisters of their family in an exemplary way but also serve them. For, service done to a pious widow is even more valuable than service to the afflicted, the helpless, the ailing and the cow. To oppress a widow, on the contrary, is most harmful because the imprecation of a suffering widow is attended with fatal consequences.

In the same way an effort should be made to relieve the suffering of others too who may be feeling miserable on any account.

(7) To make arrangements for the maintenance of dumb creatures like bulls and oxen etc., that may be suffering for want of fodder, water and shelter etc., or that may have been left uncared for by their owners due to their being diseased or old.

Similarly, to afford protection to all living beings including men, animals, birds and insects etc., to rid them of suffering and gratify them constitutes worldly service. Such worldly service too, if carried out in an unegoistic and selfless spirit, for the pleasure of God, turns into 'supreme service.'

'Supreme service' is that which rids for good a man, who has been wandering through different species of life, of all sufferings and leads him to God-Realization. While such supreme service is incessantly carried on in a habitual manner by exalted souls who have realized God, a striver can render such supreme service as a course of spiritual discipline. Although a striver lacks the capacity to bring blessedness to anyone, yet he can be instrumental in such 'supreme service' by basing their hopes on the commandments mercy and prompting of the almighty Lord and without claiming the doership.

There are many forms of his supreme service too. Here

are a few examples:—

(1) To instruct fellowmen drifting in the world in the disciplines of spiritual knowledge, meditation, disinterested action and devotion etc., on the basis of scriptures or the teachings of exalted souls so that they may be able to seek their release from the cycle of births and deaths.

(2) To read the *Gītā,* the *Rāmāyana* etc., or chant the Divine Name to a moribund person eager to hear these.

This latter service is even more valuable than the performance of a sacrifice or the bestowal of gifts, the practice of austerities and service to the needy, Japa and meditation, worship and recital of sacred texts, fellowship with saints and the study of scriptures. For, all this routine can be gone through at other times also. But the work of discoursing on topics relating to God before one who is at the point of death cannot be done after the said person has passed away. If by helping a dying man to do Japa, meditation, worship, recital of sacred texts and study of scriptures etc., and to enjoy the fellowship of saints, the mind of a moribund person gets focussed on God, he will attain blessedness instantly. The Lord says in the *Gītā:*—

अन्तकाले च मामेव स्मरन्मुक्त्वा कलेवरम्।
यः प्रयाति स मद्भावं याति नास्त्यत्र संशयः॥

(VIII.5)

'He who departs from the body, thinking of Me alone even at the time of death attains My state; there is no doubt about it."

Therefore, even if one man succeeds in attaining blessedness through our sustained efforts in this direction, our present life will have been crowned with success, because redemption of the soul is the sole object of human life. Even in the event of our failing to redeem our own self, if a single individual attains blessedness through our instrumentality, our life will have achieved its purpose. Even if we ask nothing of God, He will all the same feel disposed to redeem us, inasmuch as we are doing this work not from pride, selfishness or egotism but only for the pleasure of the Lord in a disinterested spirit. If we are born again and again and God is pleased to entrust this work to us, it would be preferable for us even to final emancipation. Therefore, whenever such an opportunity presents itself, it should not be lost. This work should be given preference over a thousand and one other engagements. For, to a man, no duty is higher than the supreme service of such a person who is exceedingly ill.

(3) To present personally or through others religious books like the *Gītā,* the *Rāmāyaṇa,* the *Bhāgavata* etc., religious periodicals like the *'Kalyan'*, the *'Kalyana-Kalpataru'*, the *'Mahābhārata'* etc., and spiritual publications such as the articles, speeches and biograhphies of exalted souls as well as their discourses, full of instructions and admonitions, on the occasion of weddings etc., to give them free to recluses and holy men and students etc., to distribute or get them distributed for the good of the people at a reasonable price or gratis; to distribute free or on payment the above-mentioned religious literature either personally or through others in Ṛṣīkulas, Gurukulas, Brahmacaryāśramas, High Schools, Colleges, seminaries and other educational institutions, jails, hospitals, Ayurvedic dispensaries etc., and to popularize them in cities, villages and suburbs, or in fairs etc., by opening shops or selling them on lorries, in push-carts or by personally carrying them in bags; these too constitute service in the real or spiritual sense of the term. This too, if carried on in an unegoistic and selfless way for the pleasure of the Lord, turns into 'supreme service.'

Therefore, everybody should take up this work of propagating spiritual literature with great earnestness and zest as a means to God-Realization.

★

God-Remembrance in the Gītā

Almost all religious-minded men of the world over glorify 'Bhajana' or remembrance of God. 'Bhajana' conveys the sense of calling to one's mind the name, identity, virtues and glory etc., of God. The word having been derived from the root 'भज सेवायाम्'; the root meaning of 'Bhajana' is to serve. Service carries the sense of personal attendance. Worship too is a part of service. Singing the praises of the Lord is also known as 'Bhajana'; muttering or chanting the name of God likewise goes by the name of 'Bhajana' and the word is also used in the sense of calling to one's mind the true character of God. In this way the silent repetition of the Divine Name, fixing one's thoughts on the divine essence, singing hymns and prayers to God, remaining engaged in service to and worship of the Deity, surrendering oneself to God and obeying His commands—all these are included in the concept of 'Bhajana.'

The Glory of Nāma-Japa is sung not only by the Hindus, but even by non-Hindus, viz., Muslims, Christians and so on. While our Muslim brethren remember Him by the names of 'Allāha' and 'Khudā', our Christian friends speak of Him as God. Whatever name of our beloved God one may repeat, it is after all only God's name. The Lord bears endless names, of which Oṁ, Hari, Rāma, Nārāyaṇa, Allāha, Khudā and God are only a few. The substance denoted by all these names is one and the same. Whether we call Him Parameśvara (the Supreme Deity), Paramātmā (the Supreme Spirit), Bhagavān (the Almighty) or by any other name, He is just the same. Some people worship God as endowed with a form, others as devoid of form, some as qualified and others as attributeless. But howsoever we may worship Him, it is Him alone that we worship; for God is manifest as well as unmanifest, both with form and without form, qualified as well as attributeless. Therefore, being all comprehensive, He is to a particular individual precisely what he thinks Him to be.

In the *Gītā,* the *Rāmāyaṇa* and the *Bhāgavata,* which are predominantly devotional in their tone, the glory of 'Bhajana' has been sung at numerous places. Besides these there are many more theistic works. God-remembrance stands glorified at the beginning, the middle as well as at the end of every scripture. In the procedure for listening to the *Mahābhārata* as detailed in the *Harivaṁśa-Purāṇa* it has been said:—

वेदे रामायणे पुण्ये भारते भरतर्षभ ।
आदौ चान्ते च मध्ये च हरिः सर्वत्र गीयते ॥

(Verse 93)

"Lord Śrī Hari, O jewel among the Bharatas, is sung in every section—at the beginning, in the middle as well as at the end of the Vedas, the Rāmāyaṇa and the holy Mahābhārata."

Now we proceed to outline below the true nature and glory of 'Bhajana' as depicted in the *Gītā.* In verses 24 to 30 of Discourse IV of the *Gītā* have been detailed a number of ways to God-Realization under the name of so many Yajñas and at the end the Lord says:—

एवं बहुविधा यज्ञा वितता ब्रह्मणो मुखे ।
कर्मजान् विद्धि तान्सर्वानेवं ज्ञात्वा विमोक्ष्यसे ॥

(*Gītā* IV.32)

"Many such forms of sacrifice have been set forth in detail through the mouth of the Vedas; know them all as involving the action of mind, senses and body. Thus knowing the truth about them you shall be freed from the bondage of action (through their performance)."

Whatever forms of Yajña there are, they all lead to God-Realization; while Japa of the Divine Name is an end in itself Lord Śrī Kṛṣṇa speaks it as His own Self—

यज्ञानां जपयज्ञोऽस्मि (*Gītā* X.25)

"Of Yajñas, I am Yajña in the form of Japa (silent repetition of the Divine Name or other sacred texts)."

Besides this, the Lord unequivocally says that whosoever quits his body and departs from this world with the monosyllable name of God, viz., 'OṀ' on his lips and with his mind fixed on the object denoted by it, viz., God, attains the supreme Goal—

ओमित्येकाक्षरं ब्रह्म व्याहरन् मामनुस्मरन् ।
यः प्रयाति त्यजन्देहं स याति परमां गतिम् ॥

(*Gītā* VIII.13)

Of the many names of God, the following three, viz., OṀ, TAT and SAT, find special mention in the *Gītā*—

ॐ तत्सदिति निर्देशो ब्रह्मणस्त्रिविधः स्मृतः ।
ब्राह्मणास्तेन वेदाश्च यज्ञाश्च विहिताः पुरा ॥

(XVII.23)

"OṀ, TAT, SAT—this has been declared to be the threefold appellation of the Absolute. At the beginning of creation, the Brahmans and the Vedas and sacrifices too were evolved by it."

It is for this reason alone that religious undertakings like sacrificial performances, religious gifts and austerities etc., are commenced with the utterance of 'OṀ' and it is further laid down that the chanting of the Vedic Mantras too should be prefixed with the utterance of OṀ. For the glory of these names, viz., OṀ, TAT and SAT, a reference is invited to the commentary on verses 17—24 of Discourse XVII, contained in the *Gītā-Tattva-Vivecanī.*

Calling to one's mind the true nature of God is 'Bhajana' of the highest order; for, whereas repetition of the Divine Name can be done even with one's tongue and breath alone, contemplation on the divine essence is possible only with the mind. And whatever is carried on with the co-operation of the mind is recognized to be the best. Hence special importance is attached to 'Bhajana' in the form of remembrance of God. God-Realization can be easily and speedily attained through it—

अनन्यचेताः सततं यो मां स्मरति नित्यशः ।
तस्याहं सुलभः पार्थ नित्ययुक्तस्य योगिनः ॥

(*Gītā* VIII.14)

"Arjuna, whosoever always and constantly thinks of Me with undivided mind, to that Yogī, ever in rapport with Me, I am easily attainable."

तेषामहं समुद्धर्ता मृत्युसंसारसागरात् ।
भवामि नचिरात्पार्थ मय्यावेशितचेतसाम् ॥

(*Gītā* XII.7)

"The aforesaid, O Arjuna, I speedily deliver from the ocean of birth and death, their mind being fixed on Me."

In this way 'Bhajana' figures in the *Gītā* at some places under the name of 'Bhajana', elsewhere under the appellation of God-remembrance and at other places under the name of meditation. We can be easily redeemed if we translate into action even one of these verses. We find it mentioned in the *Gītā* that of all courses of spiritual discipline devotion to God, that is, 'Bhajana' is the foremost—

योगिनामपि सर्वेषां मद्गतेनान्तरात्मना ।
श्रद्धावान्भजते यो मां स मे युक्ततमो मतः ॥

(VI.47)

"Of all Yogīs, again he who devoutly worships Me with his mind focussed on Me is considered by Me to be the best Yogī."

God alone is worth adoring in this perishable and transient world. The joy that is found here is no real joy. Human birth is a most rare boon. He who wallows in sense-delights turning his back on God, who is an embodiment of supreme bliss, even after attaining such a rare acquisition, is a fool. A seeker of blessedness will therefore be well advised to worship God alone at all times without break in a spirit of disinterested love and thereby make the most of his rare human birth. The Lord says to Arjuna:—

अनित्यमसुखं लोकमिमं प्राप्य भजस्व माम् ।

(First half of *Gītā* IX.33)

"Having secured this joyless and transient human life, constantly adore Me."

God gratifies every desire of His worshipper. If on any occasion He does not, even in such non-compliance on His part lies the supreme good of the worshipper. The Lord accords the foremost place to His worshippers irrespective of their motive; while He speaks of a disinterested worshipper as His own Self. Says the Lord:—

उदाराः सर्व एवैते ज्ञानी त्वात्मैव मे मतम्।
आस्थितः स हि युक्तात्मा मामेवानुत्तमां गतिम्॥

(*Gītā* VII.18)

"Indeed all these are noble, but the man of wisdom is My very Self; such is My view. For, such a devotee, who has his mind and intellect absorbed in Me, is firmly established in Me alone, the highest goal."

The Lord makes much even of the votaries of other deities and calls them His own devotees with this difference that He speaks of their process of worship as inferior to His own worship—

येऽप्यन्यदेवता भक्ता यजन्ते श्रद्धयान्विताः।
तेऽपि मामेव कौन्तेय यजन्त्यविधिपूर्वकम्॥

(*Gītā* IX.23)

"Arjuna, even those devotees who, endowed with faith, worship other gods (with some interested motive) worship Me alone, though in a wrong way."

The Lord further says that the reward attained by those people of poor understanding, however, has a beginning and an end and is perishable and that, while the worshippers of gods attain to the gods, His own devotees (howsoever they worship Him) eventually come to Him alone—

अन्तवत्तु फलं तेषां तद् भवत्यल्पमेधसाम्।
देवान्देवयजो यान्ति मद्भक्ता यान्ति मामपि॥

(*Gītā* VII.23)

We should conclude from what has been stated above that those seeking worldly gains would do better to ask these things of gods rather than of their fellow men, while it is even better to ask them of God Himself. And it is much better to ask final beatitude of God rather than worldly objects; while the best thing is to worship God in a spirit of disinterested love rather than ask anything of Him. It is such a disinterested lover that the Lord declares as the dearest to him of all the four categories of His devotees—

तेषां ज्ञानी नित्ययुक्त एकभक्तिर्विशिष्यते।
प्रियो हि ज्ञानिनोऽत्यर्थमहं स च मम प्रियः॥

(*Gītā* VII.17)

"Of the aforesaid the foremost is the man of wisdom, ever established in identity with Me and possessed of exclusive devotion. For I am extremely dear to the wise man (who knows Me in reality), and he is extremely dear to Me."

He who worships God with exclusive love is able to meet Him as he would. God cannot be attained to even through sacrificial performances, charity, austerities or even through study of the Vedas divorced from Devotion. On the other hand, He could be won according to the wishes of the devotee through single- minded devotion alone. If he seeks to behold the Lord, the latter would reveal Himself before his eyes; nay, He would confer spiritual enlightenment on him if he craves for the latter; and the Lord would grant him Liberation in the form of merger in the Lord if the devotee would have such Liberation. What is needed is that one should worship the Lord with exclusive and unalloyed love.

The Lord says:—

भक्त्या त्वनन्यया शक्य अहमेवंविधोऽर्जुन ।
ज्ञातुं द्रष्टुं च तत्त्वेन प्रवेष्टुं च परंतप ॥

(*Gītā* XI.54)

"Through single-minded devotion, however, O Arjuna, I can be seen in this form (with four arms), nay, known in essence and even entered into, O chastiser of foes !"

However steeped in sin one may be, all one's sins are wiped off through devotion to God and one speedily attains supreme peace. But one must practise 'Bhajana' in a spirit of disinterested and unalloyed love uninterruptedly.

The Lord says:—

अपि चेत्सुदुराचारो भजते मामनन्यभाक् ।
साधुरेव स मन्तव्यः सम्यग्व्यवसितो हि सः ॥
क्षिप्रं भवति धर्मात्मा शश्वच्छान्तिं निगच्छति ।
कौन्तेय प्रति जानीहि न मे भक्तः प्रणश्यति ॥

(*Gītā* IX.30-31)

"Even if the vilest sinner worships Me with exclusive devotion, he should be accounted a saint; for he has rightly resolved. (He is positive in his belief that there is nothing like devoted worship of

God). Speedily he becomes virtuous and secures lasting peace. Know it for certain, Arjuna that My devotee never falls."

He who is engaged in exclusive 'Bhajana' has been abundantly praised in the *Gītā*. God Himself protects His devotee at all times.

The Lord not only protects the man who constantly thinks of Him at all times in a disinterested spirit with full dependence on Him but He shoulders the entire responsibility of his worldly as well as other-worldly well-being—

अनन्याश्चिन्तयन्तो मां ये जनाः पर्युपासते ।
तेषां नित्याभियुक्तानां योगक्षेमं वहाम्यहम् ॥

(*Gītā* IX.22)

Total dependence on God followed by complete self-surrender to Him is equally good 'Bhajana'. The Lord vouchsafes supreme peace as well as His supreme state to him who undertakes such 'Bhajana'. The Lord says to Arjuna:—

तमेव शरणं गच्छ सर्वभावेन भारत ।
तत्प्रसादात्परां शान्तिं स्थानं प्राप्स्यसि शाश्वतम् ॥

(*Gītā* XVIII.62)

Thus it is proved that real worship of God solely consists in complete surrender to God; after asking Arjuna in the latter half of *Gītā* IX.33 to worship Him (भजस्व माम्), the Lord points out to him in the very next verse that worship of God solely consists in complete surrender to Him—

मन्मना भव मद्भक्तो मद्याजी मां नमस्कुरु ।
मामेवैष्यसि युक्त्वैवमात्मानं मत्परायणः ॥

(*Gītā* IX.34)

"Fix your mind on Me, be devoted to Me, worship Me and salute Me; thus linking yourself with Me and entirely depending on Me, you shall come to Me."

The Lord confers the highest destiny on him who approaches Him for protection, however low-born he may be—

मां हि पार्थ व्यपाश्रित्य येऽपि स्युः पापयोनयः ।
स्त्रियो वैश्यास्तथा शूद्रास्तेऽपि यान्ति परां गतिम् ॥

(*Gītā* IX.32)

"Arjuna, womenfolk, Vaiśyas(members of the trading and agriculturist classes), Śūdras (those belong to the labouring and artisan classes), as well as those of vile birth (such as the pariah), whoever they may be, taking refuge in Me they too attain the supreme goal."

Even as worship of God has been declared as consisting in seeking His protection, so rendering service to all as so many manifestation of God is equally good Bhajana. Whether a striver serves all as children of God or as so many embodiments or manifestations of God, all this is worship of God. In other words, Bhajana also means to serve all in a spirit of disinterested love as a matter of duty, realizing that God is the father and mother of all creatures, that all created beings emanate from God, that God pervades all, nay, ensouls all, so that service of God consists in serving all. As a result of this the striver undoubtedly attains the supreme goal. The Lord says in the *Gītā:—*

बहूनां जन्मनामन्ते ज्ञानवान् मां प्रपद्यते ।
वासुदेवः सर्वमिति स महात्मा सुदुर्लभः ॥

(VII.19)

"In the very last of all births the enlightened soul worships Me, realizing that all this is God. Such a great soul is very rare."

यतः प्रवृत्तिर्भूतानां येन सर्वमिदं ततम् ।
स्वकर्मणा तमभ्यर्च्य सिद्धिं विन्दति मानवः ॥

(XVIII.46)

"Man attains perfection by worshipping through the performance of his own duty Him from whom all created beings have emanated and by whom all this (visible universe) stands pervaded."

Even as a patent fire in flames is omnipresent as ether in its latent form, God too, when descending in the plane of matter as avatāra, manifests Himself as a flaming fire while pervading everywhere. Man can be speedily redeemed by reverently and lovingly paying homage, offering hospitality, rendering service and doing worship to the aforesaid Lord appearing in embodied form. One is able to attain the supreme state by rendering service and offering worship etc., to Him even when He has disappeared much more when He was bodily present in our midst on the terrestrial plane.

It is recorded in the *Vālmīki-Rāmāyaṇa* that on the occasion of Bharata's visit to the hermitage of Sage Bharadvāja, the latter in the course of his hospitality to Bharata evolved by virtue of his mystic powers a right royal palace and placed there a throne worthy of kings to sit on. Bharata, however, did not occupy that exalted seat. On the other hand, treating it as a throne belonging to Śrī Rāma, and himself holding the position of a minister, he continued to render service and offer worship to the Lord by waving a chowry the whole night:—

तत्र राजासनं दिव्यं व्यजनं छत्रमेव च।
भरतो मन्त्रिभिः सार्धमभ्यवर्तत राजवत्॥
आसनं पूजयामास रामायाभिप्रणम्य च।
बालव्यजनमादाय न्यषीदत् सचिवासने॥

(*V.Ram., Ay.* XCI.38-3

"*Bharata beheld there a heavenly throne, a chowry and a royal umbrella too. Then visualizing them as infused with the presence of King Rāma, he circumambulated all those insignia of royalty along with his ministers. Taking the throne to be occupied by Śrī Rāma he bowed low to Him and worshipped even the throne. Then holding the chowry in his hand, he went and occupied the seat intended for the chief minister.*"

In response to our mentally invoking the presence of our beloved deity and reverently and lovingly rendering service and offering worship to Him even as Bharata did at the hermitage of Bharadvāja, that night, or as a result of our rendering service and offering worship to an image or portrait of the Lord with reverence and in a spirit of disinterested love, the Lord visibly manifests Himself and accepts our service and offerings. The Lord says in the *Gītā*:—

पत्रं पुष्पं फलं तोयं यो मे भक्त्या प्रयच्छति ।
तदहं भक्त्युपहृतमश्नामि प्रयतात्मनः ॥

(IX.26)

"Whosoever offers to Me with love a leaf, a flower, a fruit or even water, I appear in person before that disinterested devotee of sinless mind, and delightfully partake of that article offered by him with love."

The Lord accommodates in His heart the man who constantly worships Him with reverence and love in a disinterested spirit under the conviction that He is more all-pervasive than ether, that there is not even an inch of space devoid of the Lord's presence. The Lord says in the *Gītā:*—

समोऽहं सर्वभूतेषु न मे द्वेष्योऽस्ति न प्रियः ।
ये भजन्ति तु मां भक्त्या मयि ते तेषु चाप्यहम् ॥

(IX.29)

"I am equally present in all beings; there is none hateful or dear to Me. They, however, who devoutly worship Me, abide in Me; and I too stand revealed in them."

Even that which may be done for winning the Lord's pleasure or for God-Realization is indirectly comprised in 'Bhajana'. Hence we should perform all our duties with the sole motive of realizing or pleasing God. Nay, we should dedicate ourselves as well as all actions being done by us to God under the conviction that everything belongs to Him, that God is ours and we are His, and that whatever is being done by us is being done under His impulse, that God is having it done by us. This too is worship of God. This naturally leads to constant remembrance of God and enables us to realize God. The Lord says to Arjuna:—

यत्करोषि यदश्नासि यज्जुहोषि ददासि यत् ।
यत्तपस्यसि कौन्तेय तत्कुरुष्व मदर्पणम् ॥
शुभाशुभफलैरेवं मोक्ष्यसे कर्मबन्धनैः ।
संन्यासयोगयुक्तात्मा विमुक्तो मामुपैष्यसि ॥

(*Gītā* IX.27-28)

"Arjuna, whatever you do, whatever you eat, whatever you offer as oblation to the sacred fire, whatever you bestow as a gift, whatever

you do by way of austerity, offer it all to Me. With your mind thus established in the Yoga of Renunciation (offering of all actions to Me), you will be freed from the bonds of Karma in the shape of good and evil consequences; and completely freed from them, you will come to Me."

Therefore, withdrawing all affinity and attachment to one's body and worldly enjoyments, one should switch it to God alone. All worldly objects are perishable and ephemeral. The wise do not take delight in them; the indiscreet alone wallow in them. The Lord says in the *Gītā:—*

ये हि संस्पर्शजा भोगा दुःखयोनय एव ते।
आद्यन्तवन्तः कौन्तेय न तेषु रमते बुधः॥

(V. 22)

"The pleasures which are born of sensecontacts are unquestionably a source of suffering only (though appearing as enjoyable to worldly-minded people). They have a beginning and an end (they come and go). Arjuna, it is for this reason that a wise man does not indulge in them."

Therefore, we should devote our time to that pursuit alone for which we have come. This human body has been vouchsafed to us neither for enjoying the pleasures of sense in the form of lickerishness, ease and comfort and luxury nor for attaining an abode in heaven. For, even those who offer worship to the gods and other heavenly beings and undertake sacrificial performances etc., with a view to attaining heaven have been declared in the *Gītā* as belonging to a lower order (See II.41—44; IX.20-21). From the above it is clear that the human body has not been vouchsafed for attaining heavenly bliss either but for redeeming the self. The man who fails to redeem his soul and fritters away his time in luxuries (of various kinds) is a fool and deserves reproach, inasmuch as he takes poison in exchange for nectar. He shall have to rue his actions bitterly in future. Therefore, we should wake up before it is too late; otherwise great harm will come to us. The Lord says in the *Rāmacaritamānasa:—*

"He reaps torture in the other world and beats his head in remorse, wrongly attributing the blame to Time, Fate and God.

*Sensuous enjoyment, brethren, is not the be-all and end-all of human existence; even heavenly enjoyment is shortlived and ends in sorrow. The fools who devote their mind to the pleasures of sense even after attaining human birth take poison in exchange for nectar. None will speak well of him who picks up a Guñjā (a black-headed red berry) throwing away the philosopher's stone."**

Just as an ailing man who takes prohibited food, mistaking it to be a source of pleasure, reaps sorrow in the end, he who indulges in sense-enjoyments, mistaking them to be a source of happiness, reaps agony. Hence we should develop a strong aversion for sense-enjoyments and should never hanker after them because no object of enjoyment can be had by merely hankering after it. No one in this world courts suffering; on the other hand everybody seeks happiness; nevertheless all have to suffer. To say nothing of other living beings, one would not find even a single man, other than a saint, who is not agonized by worldly suffering. Therefore, if anyone hankers after enjoyment or things contributory to such enjoyment, viz., wealth and house etc., one cannot have them by mere wishing. Let other things alone, one cannot even die by merely wishing to die nor can he survive at will if he so desires; for the inevitable alone comes to be. In the *Rāmacaritamānasa* we read:—

"After all, whatever Śrī Rāma has preordained must come to pass; why should one add to the complication by indulging in speculations ?"†

When everything is had as ordained by divine dispensation, why should we merely degrade ourselves by hankering after any worldly object ? It is an egregious folly to hanker after any worldly object. Therefore, giving up the desire for everything else, one should long for God-Realization alone. God alone and

* सो परत्र दुख पावइ सिर धुनि धुनि पछिताइ। कालहि कर्महि ईस्वरहि मिथ्या दोस लगाइ॥
एहि तन कर फल विषय न भाई। स्वर्गउ स्वल्प अंत दुखदाई॥
नर तनु पाइ बिषयँ मन देहीं। पलटि सुधा ते सठ बिष लेहीं॥
ताहि कबहुँ भल कहइ न कोई। गुंजा ग्रहइ परस मनि खोई॥

† होइहि सोइ जो राम रचि राखा। को करि तर्क बढ़ावइ साखा॥

nothing else is had by mere wishing; for it is we alone that hanker after material objects and not they for us. God, however, is supremely divine or spiritual and the greatest friend—unaccountably compassionate and loving to all. Therefore God too seeks those who seek him. The Lord says:—

ये यथा मां प्रपद्यन्ते तांस्तथैव भजाम्यहम्।

(*Gītā* IV.11 first half)

"Howsoever men seek Me, even so do I approach them."

How wonderful is the glory of 'Bhajana', which is reciprocated by the Lord Himself ! Nay, the Lord vouchsafes to His worshipper the light which enables him to realize Him—

तेषां सततयुक्तानां भजतां प्रीतिपूर्वकम्।
ददामि बुद्धियोगं तं येन मामुपयान्ति ते॥

(*Gītā* X.10)

"On those ever united through meditation with Me and worshipping Me with love, I confer that Yoga of wisdom through which they come to Me."

Therefore, completely surrendering oneself to God, one should always and constantly practise 'Bhajana' in the shape of ministration and worship, singing praises and offering prayers and salutations to the Lord and fix one's mind on His names and form with reverence and faith in a spirit and disinterested love.

★

The Means and Reward as Detailed in the Gītā of Developing Exclusive Love for the Lord

Exclusive Love consists in loving God and God alone to the exclusion of all others with utmost reverence and without any trace of selfishness, egotism or desire, recognizing God alone as one's own and one's all. The means of developing such undivided love and its reward have been detailed in the *Gītā* as follows:—

मच्चित्ता मद्गतप्राणा बोधयन्तः परस्परम् ।
कथयन्तश्च मां नित्यं तुष्यन्ति च रमन्ति च ॥
तेषां सततयुक्तानां भजतां प्रीतिपूर्वकम् ।
ददामि बुद्धियोगं तं येन मामुपयान्ति ते ॥

(X.9-10)

"With their mind fixed on Me, and their lives surrendered to Me (nay) enlightening one another on My greatness and speaking of Me, My devotees ever remain contented and take delight in Me. On those ever united through meditation with Me and worshipping Me with love, I confer that Yoga of wisdom through which they come to Me."

In verse 9 above the Lord points out six stepping stones to exclusive Love in the form of marks of one possessing such undivided Love, and the reward of such Love in verse 10. Now let us discuss these in some detail in the following pages.

'मच्चित्ताः'

As a man of the world remains occupied with the world all the twenty-four hours, so does a loving devotee of God remain occupied with God; and as a man of the world ever remains engrossed in the thought of the world, so does a devotee of God remain absorbed in the thought of God all the time. Invoking the presence of the Lord, aspirants desirous of meeting the Lord mentally perceive Him, speak to Him, enjoy His touch, converse with Him, worship Him, pay homage to Him, entertain Him and even cut jokes with Him. First of all the devotee invokes the presence of his beloved Deity, viz., Lord Śiva, Śrī Viṣṇu, Śrī Rāma, Śrī Kṛṣṇa or any other form of the Deity, meditates with reverence and love upon His form from toe to top alongwith His raiment, ornaments and weapons. Then with his conceptual body and with articles mentally conceived he mentally offers the traditional sixteen forms of worship to the Lord conceptually present before him. Next he extols and prays to Him considering Him as his own; and, mentally diverting himself in His company and joking with Him, remains at his house or hermitage or roams about in the woods. Wherever the Lord's feet touch the ground the earth gets charged with His magnetic influence. Hence the devotee looks upon the dust of such a piece of land as most hallowed and blessed. The bed, cushion or carpet on which the devotee converses with the Lord, taking his seat alongwith Him, gets impregnated in his eyes with divine virtues and influence. Therefore the touch of that cushion or carpet makes the hair on his body stand on end and fills his heart with rapture. Even as two friends talk with each other about love, he too likewise holds mental conversation with the Lord on Divine Love. They cast loving glances at each other. He vividly feels that the heart and eyes of the Lord are repositories of numberless Divine virtues such as equability, serenity, wisdom, love and so on; that the Lord is casting His benign look at him, in the wake of which the aforesaid virtues permeate his mind, intellect, senses, body and every pore of his skin so thoroughly that he finds himself merged in an ocean of virtues. He also feels that the objects on which the Lord casts His glances get divinized and are rendered capable of conferring blessedness. Then the devotee fancies that he is taking his meals with the Lord and that they are serving the dishes to each other, that through the touch of the Lord the food has become divinely delicious and transcendentally sweet and that as a result of partaking of that food his body is experiencing boundless gaiety, joy, tranquillity and satiety. Whatever comes into contact with the divine personality of the Lord gets charged with divine sweetness, joy, tranquillity, love and blessedness. Whatever enters the mind of the Lord is rendered capable of bestowing supreme peace, the highest joy and supreme blessedness. The Lord's personality emits a divine fragrance which is like nectar to the nose. The Lord's speech is exceedingly soft and sweet and is like nectar to the ears. The touch of the Lord's feet is like nectar to one's hands. The sight of the Lord is like nectar to the eyes. Contemplation on the Lord is like nectar to the mind. True knowledge relating to the embodied and disembodied as well as to the qualified and absolute aspects of the Lord is like nectar to the intellect. In this way the sight, touch and thought of the Lord, His speech, conversation, recreation and so on are all full of sapidity, joy, love and nectar-like sweetness. The names and forms, pastimes and the scenes of the Līlā, of the Lord are all supremely sweet, divine, unearthly and delightful. Contemplating thus, those loving devotees of God completely merge their mind in God. They have no mental bias or aptitude for anything other than God. Hence they cannot forget God even for a moment. Their mind remains constantly absorbed in and fixed on God.

'मद्गतप्राणाः'

In order to have a direct perception of the Lord in the form of their beloved Deity such as Śrī Śiva, Śrī Viṣṇu, Śrī Rāma, Śrī Kṛṣṇa and so on, such loving devotees of the Lord dedicate their life to Him, considering Him as their very life and wealth, nay, their very breath. From that time onwards, God becomes the sole objective of all their activities. They live for God and God alone. Even a moment's separation from the Lord becomes unbearable to them. They find no peace of mind without His sight. They get no sleep by night and feel no appetite by day. Nothing else than the Lord attracts them. In His absence they writhe like fish without water. As the fishes' life depends on water so their life depends on God. Smitten with the pangs of separation, love-intoxicated and mad like the Gopīs they roam about in search of God. In this way they dedicate their life and soul, nay, everything to God, or rather their all is automatically offered to God. They lose all consciousness even of their eating and drinking, speaking and moving about and so on. They have no selfish dependence on the Yakṣas (a class of demigods) or Rākṣasas (ogres), gods, human beings or animals etc., they roam about fearless of all. They lose sight even of the restrictions imposed by the scriptures and worldly usage. Having dedicated to God their mind, body, wealth, life, soul and all, they cease to have any love or affinity for anyone other than God.They solely depend upon God.

It is with regard to such loving devotees that Śrī Sundaradāsajī has sung in the following strain*—

"He does not feel ashamed of anyone in regions three, nor obeys he the words in sacred books laid down; nor fears the ghosts,

The souls of dead, nor gods, nor Yakṣas even;
Nor does he hear what other lips pronounce;
Nor sees, nor hankers after something else.
No words but praise of God his lips escape
These are the marks indeed that well describe
Devotion that has got its roots in love.

'बोधयन्तः परस्परम्'

Even as the Gopīs spoke to and enlightened one another on the essence of Divine Love, so those devotees steeped in love of God converse with their loving friends about the Name and Form, pastimes and their scene, Love, virtues and glory of the Lord and, explaining to one another their real significance and inwardness are filled with rapture and get merged in supreme unalloyed love while talking with one another about the sports and exploits as well as about the greatness of their supremely beloved Lord, as also about His sweetness, comeliness and grace, raiment and

* न लाज तीन लोककी न बेदको कह्यो करै।
न संक भूत प्रेतकी न देव जच्छ तें डरै॥
सुनै न कान और की द्रसै न और इच्छ ना।
कहै न मुक्ख और बात भक्ति प्रेम लच्छना॥

ornaments as well as about His names, excellences and glory.

'कथयन्तश्च माम्'

In the same way those devotees keep chanting the Names and singing the praises of the Lord before His loving devotees and their own beloved friends. Besides, they keep recounting through the medium of books, discourses, and correspondence etc., the truth and inwardness of the embodied and disembodied, qualified and absolute aspects of God, His exploits and divine pastimes, the glory of the Divine Name, the excellences and glory, the truth and inwardness of the eternal and supreme realm of the Lord as well as the true nature and inwardness of His endless and manifold divine and transcendent virtues. While doing so they get transported with and merged in the joy of divine Love. All the same they never get wearied of recounting them.

'नित्यं तुष्यन्ति च'

The aforesaid devotees remain ever complacent while doing all this. They regard nothing more delightful than this. Realizing again and again the truth and mysteries of God they remain sated and contented and ever remain steeped in the divine nectar of supreme peace and highest joy. They remain all the time so jolly and sprightly that even the greatest calamity cannot shake them from their joyous mood. On the other hand, they remain drunk with supreme joy while remembering the names, forms, pastimes, excellences and glory of their beloved Deity. Visualizing the loving sports and exploits of their supremely beloved Deity they remain highly gratified all the time and, realizing the truth and inwardness of His supremely delightful disposition, greatness and bodily charm, remain steeped in the highest joy.

'रमन्ति च'

Those supremely loving devotees keep sporting with the Lord Himself through unearthly and divine recreations and play. They remain constantly and absolutely revelling in God alone. They enjoy with their olfactory sense the unearthly fragrance constantly emanating from the body of their supremely beloved

Lord. This is what they call revelling in the Lord with the olfactory sense. Relishing with the palate the delightful taste of the remnants of food offered to the Lord is revelling in Him with the tongue. To fix one's eyes on the eyes of the Lord and keep feasting on the spiritual lustre in His eyes imbued with transcendental love and sweetness is to revel in Him with the sight. Touching the soles of the Lord's feet with one's hands is revelling in Him with the hands. Feasting on the sound of the Lord's anklets and the notes of His flute as also on His loving, soft and sweet speech is revelling in Him with ears. Dwelling upon the virtues, glory, bodily charm and sports etc., of the Lord is revelling in Him with the mind. And to feel enraptured on realizing the truth and inwardness of the qualified as well as of the absolute, of the embodied as well as of the disembodied aspect of the Lord is to revel in Him with the intellect. Realizing thus that fragrance of His body, the remnants of the food tasted by Him as well as His sight, touch, speech and thought etc., are all supremely sweet, enjoyable, full of love, nectarine and delightful, those loving devotees link their mind, intellect and senses with God and finding incomparable delight in feasting on His charming glances and speech, constantly revel in the Lord alone. The Gopīs cherished undivided, unalloyed and unearthly love for the Lord. Their mind and life-breath and all their activities stood solely dedicated to their beloved Lord, the wealth of their life; nay, singing His praises, they remained ever steeped in love for Him. The author of the *Bhāgavata* says:—

तन्मनस्कास्तदालापास्तद्विचेष्टास्तदात्मिकाः ।
तद्गुणानेव गायन्त्यो नात्मागाराणि सस्मरुः ॥

(X.xxx.44)

"With their mind absorbed in Him, talking of Him, imitating His various activities, nay, identified with Him and singing His praises alone, the cowherd women did not recollect their own body, much less their homes."

Loving and purely disinterested worship of the Lord consists in contemplating without interruption with faith and reverence and exclusive love on the Lord, feasting on His bodily charm, hearing

His speech and touching His feet, and realizing the truth and inwardness of His names and forms; pastimes and the scene of those pastimes, excellences and glory. Devotees who worship God as aforesaid do not seek honour, praise, position, bodily comforts and amenities, sense-delights, the wealth and dominion of all the three worlds or even final beatitude. They worship God with single-minded devotion for the sake of unalloyed love alone.

न पारमेष्ठ्यं न महेन्द्रधिष्ण्यं
न सार्वभौमं न रसाधिपत्यम्।
न योगसिद्धीरपुनर्भवं वा
मय्यर्पितात्मेच्छति मद्विनान्यत्॥

(*Śrīmad Bhāg.* XI.xiv.14)

"He who has bestowed his mind on Me no more aspires for the position of Brahmā (the highest functionary in the administration of the universe) much less for the realm of the great Indra (the ruler of paradise), still less for sovereignty over the entire globe, rulership of the subterranean worlds or mystic powers acquired through the practice of Yoga, nor does he seek (even) final beatitude (lit., cessation of rebirth for all time to come) divorced from Me."

To the devotee who cherishes such undivided and unalloyed love the Lord vouchsafes in the form of the Yoga of wisdom that spiritual insight, coupled with direct realization, which enables him to grasp aright the truth and inwardness of the embodied and disembodied as well as of the qualified and absolute aspects of God and in consequence brings him face to face with the Lord, the supreme object of his love. Once brought face to face with the Lord, he is conscious of God and God alone. He forgets even himself. When self-consciousness returns to him all his activities naturally conform like the movements of a puppet to the will and gestures of the Lord. Thenceforward all the activities of the Lord have the devotee for their objective and *vice versa*. Between them pulsates an ever new love in a uniform degree. Their mutual efforts are directed towards delighting each other, and are of the nature of a pastime to each other. Love, the lover and the beloved bear different names and forms alone; in reality, however, the three are just the same. Even as ornaments of gold have diverse names and forms, but essentially they are gold and gold alone, so God alone, who is supremely transcendent and spiritual in substance and is all love, has been called by three names, viz., Lover, Beloved and Love. In the eyes of the devotee he is the lover, the Lord is object of love and their mutual relation goes by the name of Love; while in the eyes of the Lord He is the lover, the devotee is the object of love and their relation is known by the name of love. Therefore, the entire activity of God is a sport in the eyes of the devotee and *vice versa*. Their mutual efforts are intended only to please each other.

In the realm of love no trace of shyness, pride, fear and ceremonious politeness exists vis-a-vis the lover and the beloved. In reality they are one. Hence there is no occasion for shyness, pride, fear and ceremonious politeness between them. In the relation of servant and master as well as in the domain of parental affection ceremonial politeness finds its place. Politeness and bashfulness find a place even in wifely love and shyness is found in the domain of friendliness. No trace of these is, however, found in the domain of love; for as soon as the devotee comes to be united with the Lord all the attitudes that a devotee would bear towards the Lord viz., those of a servant, friend, wife, parent and believer, appear in him. Having attained union with the Lord, who is absolute and pure consciousness and is an embodiment of supreme love and who transcends all the aforesaid attitudes the devotee too rises above them. The attainment of this supremely pure, divine and unearthly love is a mysterious phenomenon. None can describe it in words.

═══ ★ ═══